The Marshall Plan for

GETTING YOUR NOVEL PUBLISHED

90 strategies and techniques
for selling your fiction

Evan Marshall

WRITER'S DIGEST BOOKS
Cincinnati, Ohio
www.writersdigest.com

Permissions

Query letter for *Sympathy for the Devil*, cover letter for *Sympathy for the Devil*, and short synopsis of *Mumbo Gumbo*, all by Jerrilyn Farmer, copyright © 2003 by Jerrilyn Farmer. Used with permission.

Query letter for *This Pen for Hire*, by Laura Levine, copyright © 2003 by Laura Levine. Used with permission.

Synopsis of *The Grotto*, by Evelyn Rogers, copyright © 2003 by Evelyn Rogers. Used with permission.

Visit our Web site at www.writersdigest.com for information on more resources for writers.

To receive a free weekly e-mail newsletter delivering tips and updates about writing and about Writer's Digest products, register directly at our Web site at http://newsletters.fwpublications.com.

07 06 05 04 03   5 4 3 2 1

Library of Congress Cataloging-in-Publication Data

Marshall, Evan
  The Marshall plan for getting your novel published : 90 strategies and
  techniques for selling your fiction / by Evan Marshall.
      p.   cm.
  Includes index.
  ISBN 1-58297-196-X (alk. paper)
    1. Fiction—Authorship—Marketing. 2. Fiction—Authorship. I. Title:
  Getting your novel published. II. Title.

  PN3365.M27   2003
  808'.02—dc21   2003043053
                                                                  CIP

Edited by Kelly Nickell
Designed by Mary Barnes Clark
Production coordinated by Michelle Ruberg

To aspiring fiction writers everywhere

Acknowledgments

Many thanks to Jack Heffron for his enthusiasm as this project got started; Meg Leder for her work in the early stages; Donya Dickerson for her insightful comments; Kelly Nickell for her expert editing; and everyone at F&W Publications for their hard work on all aspects of this book's publication.

Thanks also to my clients and friends Jerrilyn Farmer, Laura Levine, and Evelyn Rogers for graciously allowing me to include their material in this book.

As ever, thanks to my friend and agent, Maureen Walters of Curtis Brown, Ltd., for her continuing commitment and expertise.

And thanks to my wonderful family and friends for their ongoing support, especially my wife, Martha Jewett, not only for her helpful comments and suggestions on this manuscript, but also for keeping the home fires burning while I wrote.

About the Author

Evan Marshall is the president of The Evan Marshall Agency, a leading literary agency that specializes in representing writers of all types of fiction. A former book editor and packager, he has contributed articles on writing and publishing to *Writer's Digest* and other magazines. He is the international best-selling author of *Eye Language*, *The Eyes Have It*, *The Marshall Plan for Novel Writing*, and *The Marshall Plan Workbook*. He is also the author of the Jane Stuart and Winky series of mystery novels, which include *Hanging Hannah*, *Icing Ivy*, *Missing Marlene*, *Stabbing Stephanie*, and *Toasting Tina*. He lives in Pine Brook, New Jersey. You can e-mail him at evanmarshall@TheNovelist.com, or visit his Web site at www.TheNovelist.com.

Table of Contents

Part One: Writing
52 No-Nonsense Tips for Writing Professional-Quality Fiction, With Examples From Published Novels

Part Two: Submitting Your Work
The Right Way to Work With Agents and Editors

Section I: The Product

Section II: The Pitch

Section III: The Process

Part Three: Publishing
How to Have a Long and Productive Writing Career

Genius is one percent inspiration and
ninety-nine percent perspiration.

—Thomas Alva Edison

How to Make This Book Work for You

If you've read my two previous writing guides, *The Marshall Plan for Novel Writing* and *The Marshall Plan Workbook*, you know I like to deliver the facts straight. Too many books intended for aspiring novelists present information so buried in abstract theory that readers don't know what to do with it. This book is similar to my first two Marshall Plan books in that it cuts through all the padding and gets quickly to the vital information. It's a book you can set beside your computer and refer to as you write or as you plan the next step of your career—a book you can browse through when you need a reminder about a certain point, strategy, or technique.

Why another Marshall Plan book? A couple of reasons.

First, because in the first two books I was so busy giving you information—as much as I could fit between the covers—I wasn't always able to give you as many examples of what I was talking about as I would have liked. So, in Part I of *The Marshall Plan for Getting Your Novel Published*, you'll find lots of examples, taken from novels by masters in all genres, of techniques I recommend for improving your writing—and thus improving your chances of getting published.

Second, because in the first two books I didn't have enough room to say everything I wanted to say about what to do after the plotting and the writing. Yes, in the first two books I touched briefly on writing a bang-up synopsis and approaching agents, but I still had a lot more to tell you. You'll find all that additional information in this book: information on making your writing better, and on connecting with agents and editors the right way.

One feature of this book I hope you'll find helpful is the Marshall Planners: three templates, a submission log, a quiz, and a career roadmap to help you put my advice into action. I recommend that you photocopy these Planners before you use them, so that you can use them over and over again as you work through the process of getting and continuing to be published.

Many, many of you from around the world have sent me letters and e-mails full of comments and questions about the Marshall Plan system. I thank you for the stimulating dialogue that has begun, for sharing the many success stories that have resulted from using the Plan, and simply for your kind words. I hope that in this book I have addressed the issues you have put forward. If I've left anything out, I hope you'll let me know.

Charting the Smartest Course and Evading the Obstacles to Successful Publication

It seems more people than ever want to write a book. Specifically, a novel. A blockbuster novel.

You can't really blame them. They read stories in newspapers, magazines, and newsletters about seven-figure deals made by absolute newcomers. Never mind that these stories are the exception to the rule, and that the average advance for a first novel is still under $10,000—often well under. Many aspiring writers know this statistic but don't care. *Why can't I be the exception?* they think. They can, of course, and once in a while they are. I say more power to them.

The point, though, is that whatever the reason, greater and greater numbers of manuscripts are working their way through the already overburdened postal system. At my literary agency, for example, the number of submissions has quadrupled over the past five years.

The same would go for publishing houses if most of them hadn't instituted the no-unagented-submissions rule. (This rule is, of course, partly responsible for the rise in submissions to literary agencies.)

Publishing professionals, mostly agents, must now plow through more material than ever before to find the gems suitable for publication. This means we must—and do—say no more often. It's simple math. The reality is that although the volume of submissions has increased, the number of gems, sadly, has not.

Over the past few years, speaking to my literary agent colleagues, I've come to realize that a result of this phenomenon is that we all, in a manner of speaking, are looking for reasons to say no. In the interest of self-defense and survival, we have had to find a more efficient way of separating the "glow" from the "throw" than laboriously reading everything that fills those post office baskets.

So we look for the giveaways—the telltale signs that a writer doesn't write well, or isn't professional, or doesn't have a fresh idea.

In effect, then, what gets you through the first agency or publisher door is more often than not what you *don't* do than what you *do*. That's sad, because so often a don't-do is easily corrected, a simple mistake made by someone who doesn't know any better. Why doesn't this person know any better? Because no one's told him.

I'm here to tell you—both what to do and what not to do. This entire book is made up of ideas that will help you jump those hurdles standing before the gate itself.

Once you've learned everything I can tell you to do or not to do, you'll be much farther along the road to successful publication than the majority of aspiring writers out there. My goal is to help you make it all the way.

As always, I wish you success in making all your writing dreams come true.

PART ONE

WRITING

Fifty-Two No-Nonsense Tips for Writing Professional-Quality Fiction, With Examples From Published Novels

CHAPTER 1

Viewpoint Character Writing

Viewpoint writing is writing that filters everything in your story through the perceptions of the viewpoint character of a given section (a unit of text in the Marshall Plan writing system). The reader knows only what the viewpoint character knows, sees what he sees, hears what he hears, and so on. Likewise, the reader is given only descriptions as they would naturally occur to the viewpoint character.

Describing People

There are three instances in which it's important to describe a character, and in each of these instances you do so using viewpoint writing.

■ **TIP 1:** Provide the most comprehensive description of a character at the time that character is first introduced.

But don't describe the character down to every mole and pimple; leave something to the reader's imagination. What should you describe? The characteristics that are most striking to your viewpoint character. There needn't be many; sometimes two or three details can create a vivid picture in a reader's mind. Some novelists describe a character only at the introduction and never again.

> After some minutes and the laborious rattle
> of an anti-burglar chain, the door opened
> six inches. A pair of bright eyes examined him.
> "Yes?"
> . . . Three minutes later the door opened
> wide and Mrs. Ledbetter gestured him into
> the living-room. She was well into her seventies
> with a leathery skin and a no-nonsense look
> about her. . . .
>
> *The Ice House*, by Minette Walters

Bright eyes, well into her seventies, leathery skin, a no-nonsense look. That's all we're told, but we get the picture. These are the details about Mrs. Ledbetter that our viewpoint character notices first. (Consider that what a character notices says something about that character's sensibilities, so your choice of details actually builds characterization.)

▪   ▪   ▪   ▪   ▪

▪ **TIP 2:** Describe a character when his appearance at this particular stage of your story is important.

In the following passage, Chris is captivated by Alexander, whom she hasn't seen in six years and who has grown into a handsome man. This change in Alexander is important, so Jaffe describes him.

> . . . She went downstairs, and just as she got
> there she saw Alexander coming in the door.

> She couldn't catch her breath. He was more
> beautiful than ever; changed in these six lost
> years from a boy to a man. He was wearing an
> elegantly cut dark gray flannel suit, his dark
> hair curled over his ears, and she thought:
> Heathcliff. He could be a movie star, or
> even a young diplomat, or what he was, a rising
> young banker. . . .
>
>

Class Reunion, by Rona Jaffe

■ **TIP 3:** Describe a character when her appearance has
changed in a significant way.

> At the door she paused and drew a deep
> breath. Then she stepped boldly into the room.
> "Sam—"
> Not Sam.
> Hedra.
> . . . She was wearing Allie's expensive blue
> dress from Altman's, with the silver belt,
> silver shoes, and even Allie's dangling silver
> earrings with the cubic zirconia stones.
> Transformation. Night-on-the-town time.
>
>

Single White Female, by John Lutz

In this novel, Hedra, Allie's new roommate, gradually steals
Allie's identity. In this brief passage, Lutz has shown, by
means of a few carefully chosen details, Allie's shocked reaction to Hedra's changed appearance.

Describing Places

In newbie manuscripts you often find descriptions of every room, every street, every piece of terrain—until you want to scream! Avoid newbie syndrome by keeping these tips in mind.

■ **TIP 4:** Don't describe what doesn't need describing, as in the case of places we've all been or places we've all seen.

> Cardozo arrived at Doctors Hospital a little after seven in the morning. His shield got him past the guard and he found Babe Devens's room.
> "Mrs. Devens?"
> The woman sitting in the cranked-up hospital bed gazed at him with extraordinarily large blue eyes. "Yes?"
>
> *Privileged Lives*, by Edward Stewart

We've all seen a hospital room—no need to describe it. Besides which, the room's appearance is unimportant to this section of the novel; what's important is Cardozo and Mrs. Devens's exchange.

■   ■   ■   ■   ■

■ **TIP 5:** Do describe a place your viewpoint character has never been (unless it's a place we've all been or seen; see Tip 4 above).

Use only a few well-chosen details: features your viewpoint character would notice first.

> . . . Christy went upstairs to find Nona whis-

tling cheerfully in the kitchen. The front
windows drew Christy to the tremendous
spread of mountains that rimmed the deep
cut of this little valley. Its sloping folds of
meadow showed red wherever the earth
was bare of grass, and cattle were already
browsing where green came through. Here
the trees had been banished to the high, blue-
green mountains, and to isolated clumps
that separated the houses along this ridge. . . .
    Rainbow in the Mist, by Phyllis A. Whitney

Whitney could have told us much more about the kitchen
and the view, but the details she's chosen create a complete
picture because our reader's imagination paints in the rest.

■   ■   ■   ■   ■

■ **TIP 6:** Describe a place if it has changed in an important
way.

If you take your viewpoint character somewhere she's already been, describe it again only if it has changed in a
significant way. For instance, a room may look different because furniture has been moved, or an object added or re-
moved; or it may look more opulent, or more run-down, than
when the character last saw it. A change would even include
a new feeling the character gets from this place. In the following passage, the place has changed because an important
event is going on.

Ursula, Celia and Simkin arrived home on
the day after Julian started his flight. As they

passed through Easebourne they saw Cowdray. The beautiful palace lay just ahead,
glinting golden in the sunlight, its many windows twinkling like diamonds, and they
heard gay music wafting from the colored pa-
vilions, swarming with gaily dressed folk in
crimson, green and crocus yellow.

"Why, 'tis our Cowdray festival time!" Ursula cried gladly. "I'd quite forgot."

Green Darkness, by Anya Seton

■   ■   ■   ■   ■

■ **TIP 7:** Whenever possible, work your setting description into
your character's actions.

Rather than simply telling us how a place looks, work that
description into the fabric of the story—ideally, into action
involving the viewpoint character himself.

Hendricks started eastward. The wet sand
felt crisp and cool on his feet. He walked with his
head down and his hands in his pockets, looking at the tiny shells and tangles of seaweed.
A few bugs—they looked like little black
beetles—skittered out of his path, and when
the wavewash receded, he saw minute bubbles
pop above the holes made by the
sandworms. . . .

Jaws, by Peter Benchley

The description of the beach is delivered subtly and naturally because it is woven into the action of the character, Hendricks.

■   ■   ■   ■   ■

Describing Things

■ **TIP 8:** As with describing places, tell us how something looks only if it's something we haven't seen before or if it's something whose appearance we would have no way of knowing.

If it's something we're familiar with, skip the description and just tell us what it is: a bathtub, a paperback, a window.

> He kissed her, then told the driver to take
> them to UN Plaza. His apartment was mod-
> ern and expensive, a Corbusier chaise longue
> upholstered in spotted pony skin, couches
> and chairs covered with soft black leather, the
> lights dim, wall-to-wall gray industrial car-
> peting—a powerful man's retreat. . . .
> *Punish Me With Kisses*, by William Bayer

In the above passage it's important that we get a description of the apartment. She's never seen it before, and the details Bayer gives us about it also reveal its resident's personality.

■   ■   ■   ■   ■

■ **TIP 9:** If you're describing something that is actually made up of a number of separate elements (a crowd, a flower garden, a city street), name the object first, then focus on a telling detail or two.

> ... The crowd was a motley assortment of satin-gowned ladies, languid sauntering young fops, brisk men-of-business hurrying along with an air of having weighty problems to solve, soldiers in uniform, country squires and their wives. Amber could easily recognize these latter for they all wore clothes hopelessly out of fashion—boots, when no gentleman would be seen off his horse in them; high-crowned hats like a Puritan's, though the new mode was for low ones; and knee-gartered breeches, although wide-bottom ones were now in style. Here and there was even a ruff to be seen.
>
> *Forever Amber*, by Kathleen Winsor

A crowd would have told us nothing, would have created no picture in the reader's mind. A few well-chosen details paint a whole picture and also reflect the way people actually take in large things—in small pieces.

    ■   ■   ■   ■   ■

■ **TIP 10:** When you describe an object, be specific.

Don't say a flower, say a rose or lily or daisy—as long as your viewpoint character would know what kind of flower it is (see Tip 13 on page 15). Not a boat, but a sailboat or a rowboat or a cabin cruiser or a canoe.

They went back to the little over-lived-in room
in the Hotel Bolívar. The manager was reading *El
Litoral* in the patio with his fly open for coolness. . . .
The Honorary Consul, by Graham Greene

Not just *The manager was reading a newspaper.*

CHAPTER 2

Technical Tips

Knowing What to Describe

Beginning writers frequently complain that they don't know which items around their characters to mention and which to leave out. Often, when they do mention something, it's in a way that's unrealistic in terms of the viewpoint character's perceptions. For example, a character walks into a room in which only a brief exchange with another character takes place—yet the author describes the room down to the minutest detail. This is unrealistic: in real life, a person in such a situation would get only a general impression of the room, so that's what you would give your reader. Viewpoint writing—writing that filters everything around the viewpoint character through his feelings and perceptions—can make your life much easier.

■ **TIP 11:** Mention or describe only those people, places, and things of which your viewpoint character is aware and which are important to the story.

> They wandered deeper into the woods, Sister
> Hyacinthe adding various leaves and roots to

her basket: scallions, borage, primrose and
mints. Veering off to the right to avoid a
marshy bog they came out on a clearing occu-
pied, to Sister Hyacinthe's surprise, by a long
aluminum house trailer. It fairly bristled with antennas and wires that ran toward a post; one
antenna resembled a glittering steel spider's web,
the other, a clothesline. "My goodness," she
said. "Who lives here?"

> *A Nun in the Closet*, by Dorothy Gilman

Obviously there is far more to see in the woods than what
Gilman has described. But she tells us only what's important
to this part of the story: the various leaves and roots (notice that
Gilman tells us their names, because Sister Hyacinthe knows
their names, and we are in her viewpoint); the marshy bog; the
house trailer; its antennas and wires.

■ **TIP 12:** Describe these people, places, and things in the ver-
nacular of the viewpoint character—naturally, as if the
character herself were doing the describing.

This means that if your viewpoint character is James, you
wouldn't write: *James's mother, Margery Strathmore, hurried
into the room,* because James wouldn't think about his mother
in these terms. You'd probably write: *His mother hurried into the
room,* or perhaps, if you're deep in viewpoint: *Mom hurried
into the room.*

They used to hang men at Four Turnings in
the old days.

> . . . I can remember as a little lad seeing a
> fellow hang in chains where the four roads
> meet. . . .
>
> It was winter, and some passing joker had
> placed a sprig of holly in the torn vest for
> celebration. Somehow, at seven years old,
> that seemed to me the final outrage, but I
> said nothing. Ambrose must have taken me
> there for a purpose, perhaps to test my
> nerve, to see if I would run away, or laugh,
> or cry. . . .
>
> *My Cousin Rachel*, by Daphne du Maurier

It wouldn't be natural for Philip, the narrator, to say, "Ambrose, my guardian." In the next sentence, du Maurier conveys this information in a more natural way:

> As my guardian, father, brother, counselor,
> as in fact my whole world, he was forever
> testing me.

Du Maurier has cleverly delivered important information—What is Philip's relationship to Ambrose?—by making it part of a point Philip is making.

▦   ▦   ▦   ▦   ▦

▦ **TIP 13:** If the viewpoint character wouldn't know the name of something, don't name it.

> Christ! And he was telling the truth, 'cause
> there was one of them right there, no jive,

at the back of the hall, and it looked like a half-
burnt suit of clothes lying there, kind of
vaguely in the outline of a man, and sure thing,
she could tell by the smell, there'd been a
Dead guy in the clothes, and just the sleeves
and the pant legs and shoes were left. . . .
                    The Queen of the Damned, by Anne Rice

Baby Jenks, through whose viewpoint this passage is written, isn't quite sure yet what it is she sees, so Rice simply
describes it, letting us wonder along with her character.

■ TIP 14: If the viewpoint character isn't aware of something,
don't tell us about it in a section written from his or her
viewpoint.

Examples: phones ringing, knocks on the door, people
watching. In amateurish manuscripts it's common to find
the likes of: *They slept so soundly that they did not hear the
desperate screams of the woman in the next apartment.* Remember, if the viewpoint character doesn't see it, hear it, taste it,
feel it, or smell it, neither do we.

■ TIP 15: Though it's desirable to make use of your characters'
senses in your writing, it's rarely necessary to use the actual
verbs of perception such as *saw*, *heard*, and *smelled*.

Ironically, these words distance the reader from your viewpoint character because they remind the reader that he is
not actually living the story through the character.

Simply describe the perception. Note, in the following passage, how Bob Ottum shows us what the viewpoint character sees.

> She walked back into the living room and
> picked up her skirt and her panty hose and shoes
> and then walked over to the window and
> looked down.
> The Lincoln was parked down there again.
> *The Tuesday Blade*, by Bob Ottum

Not: *She saw that the Lincoln was parked down there again.*

Section Specifics

In the Marshall Plan novel-writing system, a section is a unit of story in which a viewpoint character pursues a goal she thinks will take her closer to achieving the novel's overall story goal.

■ **TIP 16:** Don't just start your sections anywhere; get us as quickly as possible into the section's main action.

Don't take too long leading up to the meat of the section, or your readers will become bored. Give just enough setup so that the reader knows which characters you're writing about and where they are (see Anchoring the Reader on page 18), then dive into the action.

> Three days later Kay Adams got out of a taxi
> in front of the Corleone mall in Long Beach.
> She had phoned, she was expected. Tom Hagen
> met her at the door and she was disappointed

that it was him. She knew he would tell her nothing.

In the living room he gave her a drink. She had seen a couple of other men lounging around the house but not Sonny. She asked Tom Hagen directly, "Do you know where Mike is? Do you know where I can get in touch with him?"

The Godfather, by Mario Puzo

A less skillful writer might have shown Kay making the phone call, then arriving. But these details are not important to the section. The section begins when Kay comes face to face with Tom Hagen. So Puzo starts the section with Kay getting out of the taxi, then lets us know she's already phoned ahead.

Anchoring the Reader

Let your reader know right away which character you're writing about in a section. I call this anchoring the reader. It's irritating to have to have to read four paragraphs before you know which character you're reading about.

▪ **TIP 17:** Unless the section you're writing runs directly from the previous one with no visible break, state clearly in your section's first paragraph:
- who the section character is
- what time it is:
  —either relative to the previous section, if it was about the same character: twenty minutes later, that night, the following morning, or

—absolute: early Monday morning, at noon on the
sixth of September, first thing Sunday
- location

In the following passage, note how expertly Maeve Binchy
quickly anchors Father Baily in *who*, *when*, and *where*.

> Father Baily gritted his teeth when he saw
> the McMahons at Mass on Sunday. He was fast
> running out of words of consolation for the
> family. There were just so many times a
> priest could explain about things being God's
> will to a bereaved family.
>
> *The Glass Lake*, by Maeve Binchy

Updating the Reader

TIP 18: If anything important to your story has happened
to your viewpoint character since his last section, bring the
reader up-to-date right at the beginning of his new section.

> At four o'clock the following afternoon
> Samuel Weinstock leaned back in his
> chair, feeling extremely pleased with himself.
> He had sold a painting, which brought
> him a couple of weeks of relatively guilt-free
> inactivity, and the evening with Micheline
> had left him giddily euphoric. It had worked
> out just as planned: a marvelous meal,
> wonderful stories about an antique fair at
> Brussels that Micheline had just attended,

and, at the end of it, a long period of languorous, luxurious sex.

The Rembrandt Panel, by Oliver Banks

■　　■　　■　　■　　■

Conveying Emotion

■ **TIP 19:** To show a character experiencing an emotion, don't tell us about it; show the character's physical responses to the emotion.

These responses may include speech.

"Goddamnit, you son of a bitch! I'll kill you, damnit!" Jane brought her fists down sharply on the steering wheel, her screams ricocheting off the closed windows of her car. "How could you do it, you miserable bastard? How could you do that to your daughter? How could you do it?"

See Jane Run, by Joy Fielding

Nothing conveys emotion as strongly as its physical manifestations. Fielding shows Jane's anger by showing her pounding the steering wheel, screaming, and cursing her husband.

Don't say: *John was desolate* or *Ariadne was ecstatic*. That's telling, not showing, and conveys little or nothing to your reader. Convey an emotion by *showing* how the character acts with it.

■　　■　　■　　■　　■

Working With Time

■ **TIP 20:** When you need to show the passing of time, write in the summary writing mode.

In this manner you can swiftly cover a period of hours, days, weeks, even years. A few well-chosen details turn the summary into an effective bridge between passages in the active writing mode. In the passage below, the author sums up a month in his character's life by means of one sentence in the summary writing mode.

> He spent the entire month of May on an
> extended spring tour, visiting every district in the
> network, and although he was never satisfied
> that all were fully stretched, what he found
> there gave him a personal glow of achievement
> and private assurance that very little had
> been overlooked in the regions.
> *God Is an Englishman*, by R.F. Delderfield

CHAPTER 3

Section Connectors

In the Marshall Plan novel writing system, a connector is a device for connecting sections (a unit of action in which a viewpoint character seeks to achieve a short-term goal she thinks will lead her to the story goal, or in which a viewpoint character reacts to having failed to achieve the short-term goal). There are three types of connectors: space-break, run-together, and summary.

The Space-Break Connector

■ **TIP 21:** Insert a space break (press Enter twice) between two sections when:

> *A. The two sections feature different viewpoint characters:*

> Cassie sighed, and began to pour the coffee. It was going to be all right, she thought. It was going to be all right.
>
> *[space-break connector (a blank line)]*
>
> That night, Hélène went to bed on the fold-out couch in Cassie's small living room. . . .
>
> *Destiny*, by Sally Beauman

B. You want to show a passage of time and do not want to do so using summary writing (see Tip 20 on page 21):

Frank took the offered card. "I appreciate that, Bill."

[*space-break connector (a blank line)*]

Two hours later Seth Frank lifted up his phone and nothing happened. No dial tone, no outside line. The phone company was called.

Absolute Power, by David Baldacci

The Run-Together Connector

■ **TIP 22:** When you're connecting two sections of your novel that both feature the same viewpoint character, and neither a break nor any connecting text is necessary, just run the sections together without any bridging text.

I'd be careful, I said. Besides, she's never that close to me.

Sometimes she is, he said.

I looked down. I'd forgotten about that. I could feel myself blushing. I won't use it on those nights, I said. [*run-together connector (no text)*]

On the fourth evening he gave me the hand lotion, in an unlabeled plastic bottle. . . .

The Handmaid's Tale, by Margaret Atwood

The Summary Connector

■ **TIP 23:** Use a summary connector—a brief passage of relatively inconsequential action, in the summary writing mode—when you're connecting two sections featuring the same viewpoint character, don't need the drama of a space break, but need to explain what happens between the sections.

In the following passage, the summary connector is in italics:

> . . . January said she didn't know Vera and she didn't play backgammon, and she finally convinced Ned that she would be perfectly safe taking a cab home.
>
> *She fell into bed at midnight and was so exhausted that she slept. She was still asleep when her phone service rang her at eight-thirty.*
>
> "Miss Wayne, I just came on duty and I notice you didn't call in and get your messages last night."
>
> *Once Is Not Enough*, by Jacqueline Susann

■　■　■　■　■

CHAPTER 4

The Action Writing Mode

The Marshall Plan uses five different "modes" of writing: action, summary, dialogue, feelings/thoughts, and background. I'll present tips on each one in the next five chapters.

The action writing mode is the one used most in a commercial novel. It's the mode in which you straightforwardly show the story action itself.

Ordering Events

▓ **TIP 24:** Present all events one at a time, not simultaneously.

Writing so that one action happens after another makes for smoother, more natural, more professional-reading text. Even a complicated battle is rendered action-by-action by an accomplished novelist:

> [Sam] sprang out to meet Shagrat with a
> shout. He was no longer holding the Ring,
> but it was there, a hidden power, a cowing
> menace to the slaves of Mordor; and in his
> hand was Sting, and its light smote the eyes of
> the orc like the glitter of cruel stars in the

terrible elf-countries, the dream of which was a cold fear to all his kind. And Shagrat could not both fight and keep hold of his treasure. He stopped, growling, baring his fangs. Then once more, orc-fashion, he leapt aside, and as Sam sprang at him, using the heavy bundle as both shield and weapon, he thrust it hard into his enemy's face. Sam staggered, and before he could recover, Shagrat darted past and down the stairs.

> *The Return of the King*, by J.R.R. Tolkien

■　　■　　■　　■　　■

Action/Result

■ **TIP 25:** Present action in action-result order.

She looks—and sees. He bites—and tastes. She asks—he answers. The arrow hits him—he cries out. No simultaneity here, either.

> Sergeant Connolly pressed his button, and two windows were sundered from the wall by explosives. A fraction of a second later, three more windows were blown in by a wall of noise and blazing light. They flew across the room in a shower of glass and lead fragments, missing the children in the corner by three meters.
>
> *Rainbow Six*, by Tom Clancy

Sergeant Connolly presses the button (action), and five windows explode (result). The windows explode (action), and the glass and lead fragments fly across the room (result).

Writing It All Out

■ **TIP 26:** When you are in the action writing mode, don't accidentally slip into the summary writing mode. In the action writing mode, everything—even seemingly unimportant details—gets shown.

> We climbed into his borrowed Morris, and
> I introduced my daughter, Mei, who was
> going with me to the party. Again, we drove
> down Pokfulum Road, and then turned left
> through the gay uproar of the Chinese shops
> in the Saiyingpun district, past the opera
> houses, and the slums, to emerge on the
> Praya. . . .
> *A Many Splendored Thing*, by Han Suyin

Authenticity and a more vivid picture result from the author's naming Pokfulum Road, describing the "gay uproar of the Chinese shops in the Saiyingpun district," and mentioning the opera house and the slums. The summary writing mode—*We drove around Hong Kong*—would not have achieved this effect.

CHAPTER 5

The Summary Writing Mode

In the summary writing mode, you report events in a condensed, synoptic form. You tell the reader rather than show him what's going on. The summary writing mode has numerous uses.

Connecting Sections

As we've already seen in Tip 23, the summary writing mode may be used to connect two sections.

In the following passage, the summary-mode connector is in italics.

> "Of course you must!" declared Charlotte to my mother in her jovial contralto, linking her arm through her husband's. "Craven would like nothing better." She gave us all a broad wink and led him away.
>
> *We left the cool, dark theater and went out into the bright, hot, late-afternoon sun of Broadway, passing more species of humanity*

than I had ever thought possible on the way
to our parking garage.

"Was he an old friend of yours?" Mrs. Dibble asked my mother.

The Finishing School, by Gail Godwin

Reporting Events

▥ **TIP 27:** To report events whose details aren't important, use the summary writing mode.

In the following passage, the summary-mode writing is in italics.

. . . She crawled through the opening and toward the next row. Two more and they would be in the clear.

Despite the chill, she was beginning to sweat. *Anxiously she went to work on the second row. It was constructed of double strands and took almost twenty minutes to cut through. The last row was made up of triple strands, and it was forty minutes before she was finished.*

She lay on her back, gasping for breath, her arms and shoulders aching with pain.

The Pirate, by Harold Robbins

It's unnecessary to give us a blow-by-blow account of everything that happens in the summarized forty minutes, because the details don't matter. To do so would also have slowed down a passage meant to be fast-moving and suspenseful.

▥　▥　▥　▥　▥

Telescoping Time

■ **TIP 28:** To telescope time and speed up your story, write in the summary mode.

When you telescope time, you present it in a condensed form. In the following passage, the summary-mode writing is in italics.

> *Doreen spent the morning in the woods looking for a place that was suitable to hide Pharaoh, if that precaution ever seemed necessary. She returned before noon and after unsaddling the horse was making her way toward the house* when Flossie came out of the kitchen to meet her. Her eyes rolling tragically, the old woman gripped the younger one by both shoulders, seeming unable to speak until Doreen guessed her message.
>
> "My brother has come home!"
> "Yes'm!"
>
> *Look Away, Beulah Land,*
> by Lonnie Coleman

The details of Doreen's search for a hiding place for Pharaoh are unimportant. All we need to know is that she spent the morning searching. The summary writing mode was the right choice here, to telescope time but let us know what has transpired.

■　　■　　■　　■　　■

Spotlighting Emotion

■ **TIP 29:** The summary writing mode can be an especially effective means of conveying a character's emotional state.

When Seth left the Montoya party, he rode hard for an hour until he realized what he was doing to his horse. He stopped and rested. The first blind rage was gone, and the cool night air helped to clear his head of fury and liquor.

Gradually, he began to remember the way Morgan's face had lit up when she saw him, the way she had run to him. Damn that Montoya! Seth had played right into his hands, and Joaquín had enjoyed every moment of it.

The Enchanted Land, by Jude Deveraux

Deveraux doesn't give us the exact details of Seth's ride, but instead summarizes, at the same time showing us his rage by showing us how hard he rides his horse (see also Tip 19 on page 20).

CHAPTER 6

The Dialogue Writing Mode

Advance the Story

■ **TIP 30:** Whenever possible, use dialogue to show conflict between characters, as in the following confrontation.

> Deep in worried thought, I descended the concrete ramp and swung the gate door open to reenter the tunnel.
>
> Standing there waiting for me, breathing fire, was Fjbk.
>
> "What have you done to her?" he rasped.
>
> "Oh, swell," I muttered.
>
> "You must know about this! Tell me!"
>
> I thought I had seen him looking crazy before, but at this moment he looked like a total maniac. . . .
>
> *Tiebreaker*, by Jack M. Bickham

Bickham effectively uses dialogue to show us the confrontation between Brad, the novel's lead, and Fjbk, with only a brief description of Fjbk's appearance at the end of the passage.

◼ ◼ ◼ ◼ ◼

◼ **TIP 31:** Keep dialogue tight and focused.

> . . . I did not realize the extent to which it had set him off until one day he came into my office.
>
> "Hello, Robert," I said. "Did you come to cheer me up?"
>
> "Would you like to go to South America, Jake?" he asked.
>
> "No."
>
> "Why not?"
>
> "I don't know. I never wanted to go. Too expensive. You can see all the South Americans you want in Paris anyway."
>
> "They're not the real South Americans."
>
> "They look awfully real to me."
>
> *The Sun Also Rises,* by Ernest Hemingway

Hemingway, known for his economical style, does away with the inevitable chitchat that precedes most conversations in real life. He gets immediately to the meat of the discussion: whether or not Jake will accompany Robert to South America.

Tight, focused dialogue not only advances your story but also keeps it moving swiftly. Comb your dialogue for sometimes-unnecessary words like *yes, no, oh,* and *well.*

◼ ◼ ◼ ◼ ◼

The Illusion of Realism

■ **TIP 32:** Even as you keep your dialogue economical, strive to make it sound natural.

> Aretha Mae sensed something going on. She pulled her daughter to one side and said in a hoarse whisper, "You got money comin'. Real money."
>
> Cyndra was surprised. "I have?"
>
> "Mr. Browning—he came through."
>
> "Why?" Cyndra asked suspiciously.
>
> " 'Cause I told him he hadda do what's right."
>
> "I thought you didn't believe me."
>
> "Maybe I did, maybe I didn't. It don't matter—he owes you."
>
> "How much money?" Cyndra asked quickly.
>
> "We'll talk about it next week," Aretha Mae said.
>
> "Why not now?"
>
> "Now's not the time."
>
> *American Star*, by Jackie Collins

Collins gets right to the point, but the conversation between Cyndra and her mother sounds completely natural because of Collins's use of contractions, omitted words, measured use of contractions and dialect, and quick, short statements and questions.

■   ■   ■   ■   ■

Differentiating Characters

▪ **TIP 33:** Create distinctive voices for your characters to help the reader keep track of who is speaking.

> . . . When the wagon drew level again she said, "Are you going along this road?"
> "Ah."
> "How much will you charge me?"
> "Two shilling."
> "Then may I get in?"
> "Ah."
>
> *Hester Roon*, by Norah Lofts

It's not difficult to tell when Hester, the novel's lead, is speaking, and when the lower-class carter is speaking. Note that the skillful Lofts uses no dialogue tags at all in this exchange. We'll discuss tags themselves in the next tip.

▪   ▪   ▪   ▪   ▪

Tackling Tags

▪ **TIP 34:** Use a minimum of speaker tags, or attributions.

> She turns back to him. "Did you hear about Jane Kendall?"
> "Jane Kendall?" He frowns. "Who's Jane Kendall?"
> "That woman I told you about? From Gymboree?"
> He looks vacant, and she realizes that she might not have ever mentioned Jane Kendall to him after all. For some reason, though,

she's still irritated when he shakes his head
and says, "Never heard of her."

"I definitely told you about her, Joel."

Her insinuation hangs in the air between
them. He never listens anymore when she
talks to him. He doesn't think anything she has
to say is important.

"Maybe you did," he says with a shrug.
"What about her?"

"Where are you going?"

"Upstairs to change, as soon as you tell me
about this Jane Kendall person."

The Last to Know, by Wendy Corsi Staub

This passage contains only two actual attributions: *and says*
and *he says*. Staub makes it clear who's speaking, though, by
dropping a gesture between lines of dialogue (*He frowns.*) and
simply through the context of the dialogue itself. Note that
simple speaking verbs such as *said*, *asked*, and *answered* are
perfectly sufficient for most dialogue. The pros nearly always use these words or none at all.

Conversational Gestures

▪ TIP 35: Keep your characters' gestures during dialogue to a
minimum.

"Don't you think we ought to talk about
it?" she said the next morning at breakfast.

"About what?"

She looked at him; he seemed genuinely unknowing. "The conversations we've been making," she said.

"What do you mean?"

"The way you haven't been looking at me."

"What are you *talking* about? I've been looking at you."

"No you haven't."

"I have *so*. Honey, what is it? What's the matter?"

"Nothing. Never mind."

"No, don't say that. What is it? What's bothering you?"

"Nothing."

Rosemary's Baby, by Ira Levin

Levin, known for his simple, direct style, needs no gestures—or "stage business," as they call it in the theater—to add impact to what poor Rosemary and her husband, Guy, are saying. A less skillful writer might have peppered this passage with frowns, innocent looks, amazed stares, and pouts.

Breaking It Up

TIP 36: Chop up your dialogue so that no character is allowed to go on too long—unless to do so would be realistic in the context of the conversation.

Note how Jennie, a young girl, prattles on quite believably in the fourth paragraph of the following passage:

She gave my arm another squeeze, and made

a wild swoop to the right. "Hooray," she cried; "I'm going to have my picture painted."

"Won't Emily be mad?"

"Emily?" I asked.

"Emily is my best friend," she explained. "She had her picture painted by Mr. Fromkes, and I said you were going to do mine, and she said she'd never heard of you, and so I slapped her, and we quarreled."

"Well," I said. "But I thought it was Cecily you always fought with."

She looked away suddenly, and I felt her hand tremble on my arm. "Cecily died," she said in a whisper. "She had scarlet fever. Now my best friend is Emily. I thought you'd know."

Portrait of Jennie, by Robert Nathan

Keep up a quick volley of lines of dialogue between your characters. Some writers use a three-sentence-at-a-time rule, but this isn't always practical. You get the idea, though.

▪ ▪ ▪ ▪ ▪

Paragraphing Tricks

▪ TIP 37: Press Enter—start a new paragraph—whenever someone new is speaking.

Things had come to a head during the holidays. Something had occurred which had seriously upset the girl, but about this she remained silent.

"Have you tried to tell your mother how you feel about these things?"

"At first, Sir, but she never listened, so I didn't bother any more."

"Doesn't your Nan know that your being late would upset your mother?"

"Sometimes Mum's very late coming home, and Nan thinks I should not be in the house all by myself."

"Well, Pamela, there seems to be no way in which I can help."

"Wouldn't you come and talk with Mum, Sir?"

"Would that help?"

"I think it might, Sir."

To Sir, With Love, by E.R. Braithwaite

Paragraphing makes it perfectly clear who is speaking. Note Braithwaite's judicious use of the occasional *Sir* and *Pamela* to keep things straight.

■　　■　　■　　■　　■

Conveying How It's Said

■ TIP 38: Whenever possible, make the dialogue itself convey how it is spoken.

Dame Bela took no notice of her. "How old are you?" she asked me.

"Sixteen," I said, and she looked slowly all the length of me, from my bare feet to the very top of my head.

"It's to be hoped," she said, "that you've already done with growing." The way she said it made me feel fiercely hungry.

"Can you comb and spin?" she said, and first I said "Yes," remembering my mother's lies to the bailiff, and then I thought better of it and said, "No," which made the girls laugh. "But I can learn," I said. "I can learn very quickly."

"That's to be seen," said the Dame. "Show me your hands."

The Tall One, by Barbara Jefferis

In this passage Jefferis uses not a single adverb to convey how her dialogue is spoken, yet we have no trouble hearing young Mary's diffidence, Dame Bela's haughtiness.

Overuse of adverbs is another hallmark of the amateur novelist. Try to make your dialogue convey its own description. Occasionally you will need to use words other than *said* or *asked* to create the effect you want—*whispered, shouted, cried*, and so on. Or you may need to add an adverb, in cases in which there would be no other way for the reader to know how words are spoken ("You're a crafty devil," she said admiringly). Just don't overdo it.

■ ■ ■ ■ ■

Invisible Punctuation

■ **TIP 39:** Keep punctuation in dialogue simple, so that it's virtually invisible to your readers.

"What of this Welsh boy, your squire?"

"Morgan? He's been with me since he could walk, he speaks no Welsh, he's a Norman. When he's knighted I'll give him land and make him my vassal. The Welsh won't have him back."

"He's a good boy, Morgan," Roger said.

"Fifteen knights." Robert frowned, thinking. "I'm trying to remember which of them hasn't paid his fee yet."

"I'll pay them if I must. See if they will pay scutage."

"Send Simon d'Ivry," Roger said.

"Ah, no." Fulk stood up. "Simon's place, I feel, is with Thierry. If that's all, I'm going to bed."

"That's all," Robert said. "Will you be here this summer to hold court?"

"I don't know. Maybe in the autumn. I'll tell you."

"What do you plan for Simon?" Roger said.

Fulk picked up a stump of candle on the table and lit it from a taper on the wall. "I'm not sure. God will guide me."

The Earl, by Cecelia Holland

In this passage Holland uses no dashes, no ellipses, just simple periods and commas. Remember that in fiction, sentence fragments are perfectly acceptable (*Maybe in the autumn.*) and in fact are often necessary to convey natural-sounding speech.

■   ■   ■   ■   ■

The Summary Writing Mode in Dialogue: When the Words Themselves Don't Matter

■ TIP 40: Use the summary writing mode to convey dialogue whose exact words aren't important.

In the following excerpt, the passage in italics illustrates this tip.

> "It seems most efficient for you to stay,"
> Grimani said at last. "But be good enough
> not to drag this enquiry into irrelevancies. All
> right, Maestro, let's begin."
> *Donati patiently recounted how Lodovico*
> *had persuaded him to come to his villa on*
> *the Lake of Como and train a young English*
> *tenor whose identity was shrouded in*
> *mystery. . . .*
> *The Devil in Music*, by Kate Ross

Here is another example from the same novel:

> "What exactly do you mean to do?"
> *Julian explained his plan to explore the villa*
> *and its environs, and to question all who*
> *had been at odds with Lodovico Malvezzi be-*
> *fore his death, or had benefited from it. . . .*

In the two passages above, the exact details of what Donati and Julian are saying do not matter, and would only have held up the story.

■   ■   ▥   ■   ■

▪ **TIP 41:** Use the summary writing mode when a character is saying something the reader already knows.

> That cheered me up, so I went on with the rest of the stuff, about going to work and Lucy Nye dying and leaving me a house, and me getting a job in Bristol. Then I said I'd used all my money and taken work in London. Then I moved to Rutlands and met Mark and we got married. It all sounded so straight-forward that I believed it myself.
>
> *Marnie*, by Winston Graham

We already know about Marnie's fabrication and don't need to hear her deliver it again. The summary writing mode is enough here.

▪   ▪   ▪   ▪   ▪

CHAPTER 7

The Feelings/Thoughts Writing Mode

Conveying What's Thought or Felt

▓ **TIP 42:** To convey a character's thoughts, use the indirect method whenever possible.

The indirect method conveys the thought without using the thinker's exact inner words. You rarely need *he thought* or *he wondered*. The excerpt below contains examples of both indirect (in italics) and direct (in bold italics) thought used together.

> He was silent, but he didn't apologize. *Didn't she know he was guiding her to safety because she was Kusak's daughter? Not because she had once been the wife of Jiri Hrádek. She had seen through that son of a bitch eventually; perhaps she had never known how important he was in the security police.* **She's had troubles enough,** *he decided. And once, long ago, she had been his friend. . . .*
>
> *The Snare of the Hunter,* by Helen MacInnes

▓　　▓　　▓　　▓　　▓

▪ **TIP 43:** Use the direct method to convey a character's thoughts when you feel that the exact inner words of the thought will have greater impact.

In the following excerpt, only direct thought (in italics) is used.

> *Jesus,* he thought. *How could anything that made you feel so good when you snorted it put you through this much hell when you didn't have it?* Billy Joe's insides ached as if every organ scraped against the other. . . .
>
>

The Covenant of the Flame,
by David Morrell

▪   ▪   ▪   ▪   ▪

CHAPTER 8

The Background Writing Mode

Every novel must include some explanatory background passages. The trouble with background is that it stops the forward flow of your story—something you want to avoid. So you find clever ways of working background information into your story so that your reader is barely aware it's there.

Background as Explanation

■ **TIP 44:** Provide background information when it is needed to understand the story at this moment.

In the following excerpt, the background information is in italics. Metalious delivers background as explanation of the way Selena and Allison spend every Saturday, because the pattern is about to change.

> *Selena always stayed to supper on Saturdays, when Constance usually made something simple, like waffles or scrambled eggs with little sausages. To Selena, these were foods of unheard of luxury, just as ev-*

*erything about the MacKenzie house
seemed luxurious—and beautiful, something
to dream about. She loved the combination of rock maple and flowered chintz in the
MacKenzie living room, and she often
wondered, sometimes angrily, what in the
world ailed Allison that she could be un-
happy in surroundings like these, with a wonderful blonde mother, and a pink and
white bedroom of her own.*

 *This was the way the two friends had al-
ways spent their Saturday afternoons,* but
today some restlessness, some urge to con-
trariness, made Allison hesitate to answer
Selena's, "What'll we do today?" with the
stock answer.

Peyton Place, by Grace Metalious

It's necessary for us to know how Allison and Selena have
always spent their time together, in order to understand
the full importance of a change in the routine.

   ■ ■ ■ ■ ■

Minimizing Background

■ **TIP 45:** Pare down background information so that the
reader gets only what's absolutely necessary for the story
to make sense.

In the following passage, background is delivered in the
form of dialogue. Note how Signor Antonelli's explanation
is limited to the essential facts.

"What's that?" Beatrice inquired.

"The Malleus Maleficarum means 'The Witches' Hammer,' " Signor Antonelli said. "It is a tract published in Germany in 1945, written by two fanatics, Jakob Sprenger and Heinrich Krämer. It is important because it elevated witchcraft to the level of heresy, branding it once and for all as the work of the devil rather than the misguided acts of a few disturbed human beings. It offers strict guidelines for ferreting out witches and for conducting the trials of the accused."

John O'Connell was nodding in acknowledgment.

"I've never heard of it," Beatrice said.

The Witches' Hammer,
by Jane Stanton Hitchcock

Very often, accomplished novelists find ways of presenting background information through dialogue, a livelier vehicle than straight narrative.

■   ■   ■   ■   ■

Withholding Background

■ **TIP 46:** Look for ways to withhold background information in order to create a question that pulls your reader forward.

The couple shown in the following passage from Judith Guest's *Ordinary People* have suffered the loss of their son, but up to this point in the novel we do not know about this tragedy. Listening to this conversation, we know something terrible has happened, but we don't know what it is. Our desire to know, fueled by Guest's skillful withholding of this information, keeps us turning the pages.

"I don't think it's a good idea for us to blame ourselves for what happened, Cal."

"Fine," he says curtly. "Don't, then. If that means a damn thing."

Her head sinks lower. She busies herself, buttering the piece of bread in her hand.

"Beth," he says. "I'm sorry, honey. I'm sorry."

She looks up. "What's the matter?" she whispers. "Is something the matter?"

"No! Nothing's the matter."

"Then, why can't we go?" She leans toward him. "You know how good it feels to get away. All the wonderful places we've been, Spain, Portugal, Hawaii—I know it's a lot to ask, Cal, I know we have expenses—"

"It's not the money."

"—but I need it! I need to go! I need you to go with me."

"I want to go with you," he says. "We can go in the spring, maybe, any place you want."

She sits back, then, hands in her lap. "No." Her voice is flat. "If we don't go now, we won't go in the spring, either."

"That's silly," he says. "We will. I just think that now we should—this time we might try handling things differently."

"This time?"

He is upsetting her; upsetting himself, too.
And he shouldn't drink at lunch, shouldn't
have had two martinis, he is keyed up, now;
nervous. This afternoon he will sit at his
desk in a half-stupor, surrounded by a confusion of papers.

"Then, are we going to live like this? With
it always hanging over our heads?"

Ordinary People, by Judith Guest

Earlier in the novel, we have seen this same tragedy's effects
on the couple's surviving son, Conrad, without knowing
what the tragedy was.

Parceling Out Background

■ TIP 47: Whenever possible, cut up background information
and feed it to your reader in small pieces.

Not only does this method make the background information less intrusive to the forward flow of your story, but it also
helps build suspense. Your reader wants to know the rest of
this backstory.

In the following passage, the author gives us the first of a
number of incidents, which took place before the story begins, that together convey the full extent of Mopsa's madness.

Once, when Benet was about fourteen, they
had been in a train together, alone in the car-
riage, and Mopsa had tried to stab her with a
carving knife. Threatened her with it, rather.

Benet had been wondering why her mother had
brought such a large handbag with her, a
red one that didn't go with the clothes she was
wearing. Mopsa had shouted and laughed
and said wild things and then she had put the
knife back in her bag. But Benet had been
very frightened by then. She lost her head and
pulled the emergency handle, which Mopsa
called the "communication cord." The train
stopped and there had been trouble for everyone involved, and her father had been angry
and grimly sad.

She had more or less forgotten it. The memory of it came back quite vividly while she
was waiting for Mopsa at Heathrow. . . .

The Tree of Hands, by Ruth Rendell

The above passage is actually the beginning of Rendell's
novel; she has used this bizarre piece of background as her
story's hook. It raises questions in the reader's mind, questions
that the reader must read further to find the answers to.

Disguising Background

■ TIP 48: Whenever possible, convert background into the
action, dialogue, or feelings/thoughts writing mode.

. . . "Oh, Eleanor, what is all this? Why did
you send for me so secretly? And it's been
so long . . ."

He took her hand and brushed it with his

lips as he realized that, after so long a separation, they had hardly greeted one another, that her first words to him had been a warning of danger. "What has happened?" he asked again.

"So many things," she said heavily. "Terrible things, Richard. Perhaps it was wrong of me to send for you . . . but I couldn't bear for you to hear it all from the lips of a casual gossip. And I've been virtually a prisoner ever since . . . ever since . . . " Her voice broke and Richard reached out a comforting arm which she ignored. "Sit down, dear heart, and I'll try to tell you everything. You would do well to drink some wine . . . pour for me, too. Richard, the first thing is . . . my father is dead. He died six weeks or more ago, in Compostella."

Eleanor the Queen, by Norah Lofts

Lofts has used dialogue to incorporate important background information into this scene at the beginning of her novel, lacing it with clues about a past relationship between Eleanor and Richard. The combination makes the background more palatable and draws the reader along.

Flashbacks in a Flash

■ TIP 49: Use a flashback when the exact details of a background incident are important enough that the incident must be presented blow-by-blow.

In the following passage, the flashback—a passage of dialogue from Ambrose—is in italics.

> He reckoned without his health, though,
> and when school and university lay behind
> me it was then his turn to go.
> *"They tell me if I spend another winter being*
> *rained on every day I shall end my days crippled in*
> *a Bath chair," he said to me. "I must go off and*
> *search for the sun. The shores of Spain or*
> *Egypt, anywhere on the Mediterranean where it*
> *is dry and warm. I don't particularly want to*
> *go, but on the other hand I'm damned if I'll end*
> *my life a cripple. There is one advantage in*
> *the plan. I shall bring back plants that nobody*
> *else has got. We'll see how the demons thrive*
> *in Cornish soil."*
> *My Cousin Rachel*, by Daphne du Maurier

Here it is important to the author for us to hear Ambrose's exact words during this episode that takes place before the novel's start.

Be sparing with flashbacks, avoiding them when at all possible. They so successfully stop a novel's forward progress that some editors forbid their authors to use them. Here, you'll notice that du Maurier kept the flashback brief.

■　　■　　■　　■　　■

CHAPTER 9

Writing Dramatically

When a passage in a novel gives you that wonderful frisson that only beautifully written fiction can give you, it's because the novelist has utilized any of a number of tricks that add drama and emotional impact to the text. Here are some of those tricks for you to use in your own writing.

Word-Placement Savvy

■ **TIP 50:** Remember that the end of a sentence carries the most emphasis.

> "Last night I dreamt I went to Manderley again."
>
> *Rebecca*, by Daphne du Maurier

The word *again* is at the end of the sentence because du Maurier wanted to stress the idea of Rebecca dreaming that she had gone back to that place of such tragedy. Would this sentence be as powerful if du Maurier had written *I dreamt I went to Manderley again last night*?

Savvy novelists often like to add a touch of drama at certain points in their novels, particularly at the places where readers typically pick books up and put them down (act closers), by creating a sentence whose most dramatic word or words come at the end.

Where can you make use of this technique most effectively? The first sentence of your book:

> Call me Ishmael.
> *Moby Dick*, by Herman Melville

The first sentence of a section:

> In the bright Sunday-morning sunlight, on the dirt road leading to the famous Church of the Blessed Virgin Mary, a huge white horse cantered slowly.
> *Omerta*, by Mario Puzo

The last sentence of a section:

> "What are you doing, Sandy?" said Miss Brodie.
> "Only playing," said Sandy, photographing this new Miss Brodie with her little eyes.
> *The Prime of Miss Jean Brodie*, by Muriel Spark

The first sentence of a chapter:

> Joanne stares around the room at the small collection of mourners.
> *The Deep End*, by Joy Fielding

The last sentence of a chapter:

> I rolled over and looked at Jonathan. Jona-
> than looked at me. I got out of the bed and went
> into the bathroom and fixed up. I am not com-
> pletely mad.
>
> *Diary of a Mad Housewife*, by Sue Kaufman

The last sentence of your book:

> It was a far cry from Kensington, a far cry.
>
> *A Far Cry From Kensington*,
> by Muriel Spark

When to Break the Action/Result Rule

TIP 51: To show a character's reaction to something shocking, break the action/result rule and show the reaction before describing what is being reacted to.

Got that? Let's back up a little. In good fiction writing,
actions create results. A character speaks; another character responds. A bullet hits a character; the character screams.
A character looks out a window; the character sees what's
out that window.

Now that you know the rule, I'm going to tell you one instance
in which it's okay to break it: when a character suddenly
discovers something heartstoppingly shocking. In this case, you'll
create a more dramatic effect if you have your character react
first, then describe what it is he has seen. This technique works
for a couple of reasons. First, a tiny moment of suspense is
created between the horrified reaction and the description of

what's being seen; the reader's eyes open wider and move quickly onward to learn what's there. Second, a truly awful spectacle will most likely require a good amount of description. If you describe the spectacle at length, then show your character's reaction, there's the danger of creating an odd, delayed-reaction effect that is not desirable.

> . . . Across from her the door that led to
> Hydrotherapies was just closing. Its latch clicked
> softly and she saw the knob released from the
> other side by an unseen hand. She opened
> her mouth to call out but as she stepped for-
> ward the beam of her flashlight dropped
> and she gasped in horror.
>
> Marcel lay in the pale green tub, his eyes
> turned vacantly to the ceiling. Blood spat-
> tered the sides of the tub and ran in zigzag lines
> across his white jacket. His throat had been
> cut from ear to ear.
>
> *A Palm for Mrs. Pollifax*,
> by Dorothy Gilman

Cliffhangers

TIP 52: Keep your readers flipping the pages by using cliffhangers.

The smartest novelists use this old trick of keeping readers hanging at the end of a passage, forcing them to read on to learn what happens. A cliffhanger is any device that leaves the reader wanting to know more; for example, a character about to embark on a dangerous mission, a line of provocative dialogue, or a door beginning to swing open in a darkened room. Use this technique in all of the following places in your novel.

At the end of a section:

> She thought about Nick in New York about
> to get his big chance. She wasn't planning
> on playing the little sister role, dragging along
> behind. She had every intention of making
> it just as big as he.
> "Mr. Lee—"
> "Call me Marik."
> "Marik. Tell me the truth—do Reno Rec-
> ords and I have a future together, or am I
> wasting my time?"
>
> *American Star*, by Jackie Collins

At the end of a chapter:

> "I do sympathize with you," Chips said.
> "I hoped you would. And that brings me to
> what I came here to ask you. Briefly, my
> suggestion is that—if you felt equal to it and
> would care to—how about coming back
> here for a while? You look pretty fit, and, of
> course, you know all the ropes. I don't
> mean a lot of hard work for you—you needn't
> take anything strenuously—just a few odd
> jobs here and there, as you choose. What I'd
> like you for more than anything else is not
> for the actual work you'd do—though that,

naturally, would be very valuable—but for your help in other ways—in just belonging here. There's nobody ever been more popular than you were, and are still—you'd help to hold things together if there were any danger of them flying to bits. And perhaps there is that danger. . . . "

Chips answered, breathlessly and with a holy joy in his heart: "I'll come. . . . "

Good-Bye, Mr. Chips, by James Hilton

PART TWO

SUBMITTING YOUR WORK

The Right Way to Work With Agents and Editors

Section I

THE PRODUCT

CHAPTER 10

Timing: What to Show When

They say timing is everything. In your quest to get your novel published, timing isn't everything, but it counts for an awful lot.

Let me explain. A writer signs up for a one-on-one appointment with an agent at a writers conference. After the introductions, the agent asks the writer to tell her about his project. The writer begins by saying that he is only a couple of chapters into his novel, but wanted to run the idea past the agent to see if she would like to read the book when it's finished—which the writer estimates will be in about a year. The writer has a rough synopsis with him, though; would the agent like to give it a quick once-over while they're sitting there?

The agent's eyes have already glazed over; she politely declines the outline, saying she wouldn't be able to concentrate on it right now. In truth, she's thinking, *Bad timing!* First of all, the writer shouldn't have bothered making an appointment until his novel was completed. That's because if the agent had expressed interest in it, he could have sent it to her as soon as he got home, so it would have been waiting for her when she returned to her office. Then there would have been a very good chance the agent would have remembered this writer, and that she would have remembered the writer's description of his story and was still interested in or excited about it.

A writer who tells an agent about his or her novel and submits it a year, six months, or even a month later runs a strong risk of having been dropped from the agent's already overburdened memory bank. Moreover, agents' needs are constantly changing. One month an agent may be looking for a certain type of novel; the next month he may be overloaded with them. One month the agent may not be looking for new clients; the next month he may be actively seeking them. One month the agent may be in business; the next month he may have become a sheep farmer in Wisconsin. Moral: Strike while the iron is hot! When someone wants to see your book, or part of it, or a proposal for it, send it *now*.

What else has this writer done wrong? By using his appointment to talk about a book that isn't finished and to get the agent's opinion on a synopsis with no novel behind it, he has in effect tried to use the agent as a free consultant. That's not why agents take these appointments. They take them to hear about books that already exist and ask to see the ones they think they might be able to sell. Once a writer has become an agent's client, it's perfectly appropriate for the writer to ask the agent for feedback on material. The writer in the above scenario, on the other hand, has abused his appointment, wasted both his and the agent's time, and most likely alienated her to boot. And it's all because of bad timing.

In this chapter, I'll tell you about good timing—what material to show to whom at what point for optimum results.

Advice for Everyone

I'll be addressing various situations and how to make the best of them, and in each of these my advice may differ; but here's one piece of advice that applies to every writer: Before you make any kind of contact with an agent or an editor, *finish your novel*. By "finish," I mean edit it, polish it, print it out, put it in a box, and literally have it ready to submit. You've done your very best work; the book is the best you can make it. I don't mean you're a few chapters from completion, you're about to do the final edit or polish, or you've got two possible endings written and are trying to figure out which one to go with. (Can you tell I've heard all this before?) I mean *finished. Done.*

Yet even now you're not ready for the next step. You should now prepare both a short-form and long-form synopsis of your novel (see chapter eleven).

Now you're ready for the next step.

Making Contact

Now you're ready to start reaching out to the publishing people who can help get your novel into print: agents and/or editors. There are several ways to do this.

In chapter fifteen, I discuss the process of actually targeting the right agents for you and your work. Here we'll assume that you have already gone through this process (perhaps while you were still writing): You know which agents are right and you're ready to contact them. There are basically two ways to do this.

Writers Conferences and Other Personal Encounters

As you'll see in chapter fifteen, a writers conference is an excellent place to meet agents. When you register for a writers

conference, you are usually given the opportunity to sign up
for a brief (usually ten to twenty minutes) appointment
with your choice of one or more agents who will be attending
the conference. (Sometimes on the first day of a conference
an appointment sign-up sheet is posted. If this is the case, be
sure to get there early to get an appointment with the agent
or agents you really want to see.)

The day of the conference finally arrives and it's time for
your appointment. Let's talk for a minute about why you're both
there.

The agent has come to the conference to get exposure (you'll
often find newer, hungrier agents at conferences—a good
thing); to share his or her expertise with attendees by presenting a talk or workshop, or sitting on a panel; and most
importantly, to find writers to represent.

You're at the conference to enjoy the company of fellow
writers; to learn from agents', editors', and published writers' presentations; and, perhaps most importantly, to meet one
or more agents interested in reading your novel.

What will you be presenting to these agents? First of all,
you! So you want to make your best impression. Some
agents may not care how you look, but others will—and since
you don't know the tastes of the ones you'll be meeting,
assume they all care. This means jeans and a T-shirt or sweat-
shirt won't cut it. Think business casual, and (I know I
don't have to tell you) clean hair, gleaming teeth, fresh breath.
Pen and paper are also important, for reasons you'll see
soon.

Now, back to your novel. *Do not* take the manuscript to
the conference. Many writers make this mistake, thinking
they can somehow entice an agent to take the manuscript back

to the office, or even to read it during the conference itself. We couldn't fill our luggage with manuscripts even if we wanted to. But we don't want to.

I have attended dozens and dozens of writers conferences during my years as an editor and an agent, and I think I've seen it all. Writers have left me letters at the front desk, asking to rendezvous at a certain place at a certain time to discuss their novels. Writers have called my hotel room at midnight to ask if they could buy me a drink—and discuss their novels. Women have flirted with me, even propositioned me. Men have followed me into the men's room and slid manuscripts under the stall door; others have brought up their work while standing at the next urinal. I know it sounds like a funny movie, but it's true, and it's not funny. It's rude and unprofessional, not to mention that it casts these writers in a desperate, unsavory light.

I hope I've convinced you not to have your manuscript snuggled into a corner of your suitcase when you attend the conference.

So what *do* you show? Something not usually committed to paper. Your pitch.

The Pitch

What is a pitch? It's a brief, powerful oral description of your story. Think Hollywood pitch session. You've only got a few minutes, so you want to be prepared to do it right.

In the nonfiction world we often hear that it's necessary for an author to have an "elevator speech"—a quick, punchy description of his or her book—always ready.

The pitch is an elevator speech for a novel. It has to be short, not only because you won't have much time to present it, but

> **HELPFUL HINT:** When you attend a writers conference, sign up for an appointment with as many agents as possible who handle fiction. You never know which one will get most excited about your story idea. Pitch to them all, and if they all get excited, send material to them all, being sure to inform them that they are being included in a simultaneous submission.

also because you've got to memorize it. But the best reason is that you want your story to sound "high concept," a Hollywood term for a story that has a grabby, commercial premise or gimmick—the "hook." If you've read my books *The Marshall Plan for Novel Writing* and *The Marshall Plan Workbook*, you know I believe it's important that your novel be high-concept. If you can't come up with your novel's hook or high concept for your agent pitch, you may need to go back to your novel to make sure its story idea is as powerful as it can be.

The pitch itself consists primarily of the conflict inherent in your lead's main story line. One way to discern your novel's best pitch is to ask yourself: Who are the lead and the lead's opposition, and how do they clash? In what context? The pitch isn't your entire story by any means; it's the setup. It's how *TV Guide* might describe it if it were a movie being shown on television.

Here are possible pitches for a few already published novels.

A woman moves with her husband and children from New York City to an idyllic Con-

necticut town, only to learn that husbands are
having their wives turned into automa-
tons—and she's up for conversion soon.
The Stepford Wives, by Ira Levin

A man seeks to overcome family abuse and
his anger and resentment toward his para-
noid-schizophrenic twin brother in order to
put his life back together.
I Know This Much Is True, by Wally Lamb

A poor beauty sets out to win an earl's prizes
to finance her beloved nanny's operation,
only to find the earl determined to win her love.
The Incomparable, by Barbara Cartland

How do you present your pitch? First, try to stay calm. For
many writers, this appointment is their first face-to-face
encounter with someone who actually works in the publishing
industry. Writers have been known to sweat, stutter, or
become tongue-tied in this situation.

There's no need to be nervous. Remember that the agent is
just a person, like your doctor or dentist or lawyer or
brother or spouse. He possesses no magical powers and is no
better than you. In fact, should you and the agent ultimately work together, the agent will be working for you!

So, keeping in mind that this person is a professional just
like you, politely introduce yourself, take a seat, and tell
the agent you're here to talk about the novel you've completed.
Tell the agent your novel's genre, its title, and its word
count (see page 83). Then say something like, "Here's the story

HELPFUL HINT: If you're like me, your mouth goes dry in tense situations. Carry a small bottle of mineral water with you to your agent and editor appointments. Everyone's used to seeing these and won't think twice when you take a discreet sip.

in a nutshell . . . " and deliver your pitch, which you've taken time to memorize so that you can deliver it smoothly and error-free.

The best reaction you can hope for is excitement on the part of the agent. But even if you get only a restrained eyebrow lift, a silent nod, or a courteous "Go on," be ready to go into more detail about your story. After all, your pitch won't take up the whole appointment, even if you get only ten minutes.

The agent may ask you specific questions, or you may simply be encouraged to continue. Either way, present more pertinent story details—setting, time period, any particulars you think are especially appealing or relevant to current events or current reading tastes.

You won't want to use all of your allotted time describing your story; usually this description should take up about a third of the session. Tell the agent anything about yourself that's relevant to the novel. Perhaps you have had an experience the story is drawn from, or worked in the industry in which the story takes place.

Present any other pertinent credentials: writing organizations you belong to, previous writing credits.

If applicable, mention plans you may have to turn this novel into the first of a series, or a trilogy, or simply a succession of books in the same genre.

You can even say you believe your novel will appeal to fans of a certain writer or writers if you feel doing so will present your story in a more positive light and give a sharper idea of the book itself.

Don't "review" yourself. By this I mean don't praise your own work in any way. It goes without saying that you value your work highly, and self-praise is amateurish.

When you're finished speaking and have answered all of the agent's questions, don't be afraid to simply come right out and ask, "May I send you my novel?" After all, that's why you're there.

The goal, of course, is to get a resounding yes, but if you don't, smile and thank the agent for his or her time. There will be other conferences, other agents.

If, on the other hand, the agent does say yes, be sure to find out exactly what he would like to see. Agents' preferences vary considerably. Many like to start with a synopsis and the first three chapters. I happen to prefer to receive the entire manuscript. Whatever the agent says, write it down. If he hasn't handed you a business card, say, "I know you're listed in the directories, but could you please confirm your mailing address?" Write this down.

Good work! You've handled yourself well. You've either gotten a yes out of an agent or at the very least made a good impression. Who knows? You may someday want to meet with this agent again about another novel, and he may remember you—favorably, of course.

If you got a yes, package up your material—whatever the agent asked to see—along with a cover letter (see page 104)

HELPFUL HINT: Sometimes the best times to chat with an agent are during icebreakers or at lunch or dinner. See if you can't subtly position yourself next to an agent you're interested in talking to. Be friendly—not openly eager—or the agent or editor will make tracks. Toward the end of your time together, put out your hand and say you've enjoyed chatting . . . and would it be all right if you sent your novel along for consideration? I've agreed to look at a number of manuscripts under these circumstances—and took on several of their writers!

and self-addressed stamped envelope, and send it off as soon as you get home. You'll find instructions on packaging and mailing your material in chapter eleven. It's important to follow up in a timely manner so that the agent will still remember and be interested in your work.

Now you wait. How long? If two months pass without a response, you should probably cross this agent off your list (see page 156 for the Marshall Planner: Submission Log). Either he has read your material, isn't interested, and hasn't bothered to tell you so; or he is so busy he (or his reader—yes, agents, like editors, often use readers to screen material) hasn't had a chance to read your submission. Either way, this person is probably not right for you.

If you have sent only a synopsis, or a synopsis and sample chapters, you may get a letter, a phone call, or an e-mail from the agent or his secretary or assistant asking to see your entire manuscript. If you do receive such a message, send the manuscript immediately, again including a self-addressed, stamped envelope and a cover letter (see page 104), worded appropriately for this situation. Again, follow the two-month rule.

> **HELPFUL HINT:** It's tempting to toss additional goodies into the submission package. The bonus item agents receive most often is the author's photograph. Invariably these photos depict attractive people. It's clear these writers believe that being attractive is a plus—and this is true, *if* the writer also has talent. At this stage, before your manuscript has even been considered, it's bad form to enclose your photo or anything else. Resist the urge to add items that will mark you as an amateur.

If, at any stage of the submission process, you receive a no (sometimes this will be in the form of a printed rejection slip; other times, if the agent thinks you show promise, in the form of a personalized letter), move on to another agent, either one you've met at a conference or one you've targeted in your agent research (in the latter case you'll send a query letter; see page 81).

Is it all right to send your material to more than one agent at a time? Many agents nowadays require exclusive submissions. Most of these agents will state this requirement in their directory listing (see page 131). If an agent you feel strongly is right for your book asks to read it and requires exclusivity, be sure to find out for what period of time (it varies according to the agent), then decide whether waiting that long without submitting to other agents is worth it to you. If you agree to an exclusive submission, a polite letter or phone call is perfectly acceptable if you've had no response by the end of the agreed-upon time period.

Let's say your material is already on submission with one or more agents and a new agent you've queried or met at a writers conference agrees to read your work, but only on an exclusive basis. If you would like to submit to this agent, simply wait until the other agents have responded and (if you're still agent-hunting) submit to the new one. Don't send a letter explaining that your manuscript is being considered by another agent, but that if that agent rejects it, you'll send it right along. That's like saying to a boy who has just asked you to the prom, "I'm hoping Joe will take me, but if he decides not to, I'll go with you." How would *you* like that? In this case, discretion is the better part of valor.

What if you want to submit to several agents, none of whom requires exclusivity? I say that's fine, as long as you play fair and let each agent know you're submitting simultaneously. It's also a good idea to say something along the lines of, " . . . however, I will not select an agent until I have received everyone's response." Then each agent knows that although he is in competition (a good thing—it'll make him put your material in or near the top of his reading pile), if he wants to represent you, you won't make a decision before allowing him to make his case. The agent will know he won't be investing time to read your manuscript (or investing money to have it read), only to have it yanked away by a competitor without notice.

Here's the best "what if" of all: What if several agents offer representation? As my grandmother might have said, "We should all have such problems." It's not a problem at all, of course. You've played fair and notified these agents that they were reading a simultaneous submission. Now, based on your conversations with these agents, select the one you feel will do the best job for you and send the others courteous letters thanking them for their time and interest and saying you have accepted other representation.

Meeting Editors

You're just as likely to meet editors at writers conferences as you are to meet agents. Editors, too, often grant one-on-one interviews, except that they do not always do so because they are seeking submissions. Sometimes they agree to interviews as an accommodation to the conference and all they can offer writers is advice, since they do not accept unagented submissions. If your research tells you that an editor at a writers conference you're attending publishes the kind of novel you've written, *and* he's open to unagented submissions, by all means make an appointment. Follow the same rules as for agents, above.

HELPFUL HINT: If you attend a writers conference before your novel is completed, why not make an appointment or two with an editor who is meeting with writers not necessarily to find manuscripts but to give advice? Under these circumstances it's perfectly acceptable to run your story idea past the editor and get some free feedback. That's why the editor is there!

Other Encounters

What if you meet an agent or an editor somewhere other than at a writers conference? It can happen. Agents are people, just like you, and are likely to pop up at a party, in the supermarket, or at the gym. If you believe that this agent could be right for your novel, find the right moment to politely ask to submit to him. It's likely you'll get a yes. Be sure to ask exactly what the agent or editor would like to see. Send this, with a cover letter (see page 104) and SASE immediately.

The Query Letter and When to Send It

The query letter is the most commonly used method of making contact with an agent or editor (yes, you can approach some editors directly; see chapter fourteen). I go into detail about preparing the query letter in chapter eleven, and provide examples in Appendix A. Here we're talking about timing. Once you've done your homework about agents (see chapter fifteen), it's time to prepare your query letter. You'll find the nuts and bolts of query letters in the following chapter.

If you have not yet published a novel with a commercial (as opposed to a subsidy or cooperative) publishing company, or if you have only self-published, you should not query agents until your novel is completed and polished to the best of your ability, *and* you have created short and long synopses of your novel as well (see pages 98 and 89, respectively).

Quite often at my agency I receive query letters from unpublished writers, asking to submit portions of their unfinished novels, or asking if I would be interested in seeing a book they plan to finish next month, in a few months, or in a year. If you aren't yet published, you're going to have to submit an entire manuscript, and it's only good sense not to start talking to people about it until it's ready to send. Chances are good that an agent or editor won't take your query very seriously if your book isn't finished; but what if an agent or editor does agree to look at your work? By the time you're ready to send it, he probably won't remember you! If an agent or editor responds positively to your query, you want to be able to respond immediately.

How long should you wait for a response? Six weeks is long enough for any professional to respond to a one-page letter. If an agent you've queried hasn't responded after this amount of time, consider yourself rejected and cross this agent off your list.

Can you query numerous agents simultaneously? Sure. Why? Because with your brief query letter, you are only soliciting interest—entirely different from sending a large number of agents your manuscript without letting them know they have competition. Must you tell them you are querying simultaneously? I wouldn't. If you get more than one positive response at a time, simply follow the guidelines above for simultaneous submission of material.

Again, agents' preferences vary. One may request a short synopsis (see page 98 and Appendix D), another a longer synopsis (see page 89 and Appendix C), another a synopsis (short? long?) and sample chapters, another a synopsis (short? long?) and the complete manuscript, yet another just the manuscript. Whatever the agent requests, you'll have it ready and will send it off right away, always enclosing a courteous cover letter (see page 104) and an appropriately sized SASE.

Speaking of preferences, before you approach an agent or

editor you haven't met, be sure to check a directory like *Writer's Market* to see if she has any special preferences. Though the most commonly accepted form of first approach is the query letter, some agents and editors request other materials. Needless to say, their preferences are what you should follow.

Now that we've discussed the timing of submissions, we need to talk about the submissions themselves. We'll cover the query letter, the cover letter, and the synopsis in chapter eleven. We'll cover preparation of the manuscript itself in chapter twelve.

CHAPTER 11

The Fiction Proposal—The Way Agents and Editors Like Best

What is a fiction proposal? It's any tool that helps sell your novel. In a way, a pitch is a form of proposal. However, in this chapter we'll discuss the *written* forms of fiction proposals: the query letter, the synopsis (a detailed summary of your novel), the short synopsis (a one- to six-page summary), and the cover letter.

The Art of the Query

The universally accepted method of approaching a literary agent or an editor is by means of a query letter (a brief business letter that describes your project and asks the agent or editor if he's willing to consider your manuscript), or, if you have already published a novel, your proposal.

When must you query an agent or editor about a *complete manuscript* rather than a proposal?

1. If you have never had a novel published by an established, commercial (as opposed to a subsidy or cooperative) publisher.
2. If you have published only nonfiction. Many writers

who have had nonfiction books published make the mistake of believing that a nonfiction credit will allow them to submit only a proposal for a novel. The reality is that agents and editors have seen over and over again that proficiency in nonfiction does not guarantee proficiency in fiction.

3. If you have self-published a novel (whether in print or e-book form). Agents and editors don't count this for much, so the above rules apply. However, if the self-published novel itself is the project you would like an agent to sell to a major publisher, follow the guidelines above as for a manuscript. Today it is not unusual for a self-published book to sell to a commercial publisher, which republishes it to reach a far broader market.

4. If you have published only short stories. This credential may make you more attractive to agents and editors, but you should still refrain from contacting them until your novel is complete, polished, and ready to send at a moment's notice.

When is it all right to query an agent or an editor about a *proposal* rather than a complete manuscript? If you have published one or more novels with an established commercial publisher. Send a query letter without other material, unless you have good reason to believe the person you're contacting prefers otherwise (for instance, if his directory listing asks for a query letter and short synopsis).

Whatever your situation, have both a synopsis and short synopsis ready to submit along with your novel, so that you'll be ready when you receive positive responses to your queries. It can't hurt to have your cover letter ready, too. Remember that when you receive positive responses from agents and editors, your submission packages will vary, since some agents and editors like to take the process in stages—first a query letter, then a synopsis or a synopsis and sample chapters, then the complete manuscript—while others like everything at once. As I've said before, send exactly what's requested.

First Impressions

Before we go into the dos and don'ts of writing the query, let's take a moment to think about its function. In most cases it's your first contact with an agent or an editor. It makes sense, then, not to rush this important tool, to take the time necessary to make it your best work rather than dashing something off in the excitement of submitting.

My agency, like all agencies, receives numerous query letters daily. My secretary opens them and piles them on a corner of my desk. I set aside about ten minutes a day to review these letters, because that's about as long as it takes—even when there are twenty or more of them. Why? Because I can tell at a glance which ones I'm not interested in. How? They contain grammatical errors, inappropriate or irrelevant comments (which immediately make agents like me, who have seen it all, draw back like a vampire from garlic); and more to the point, they are poorly written. If someone can't write a query letter, what are the chances of an entire novel by this person having any merit? I know what you're probably thinking: Some talented novelists just aren't good at writing queries. Maybe, but it's a chance I'm willing to take.

So how do you write the best possible query letter? Let's

assume, first, that you have done your homework and are as certain as you can be that you are approaching the appropriate people.

Query Letter Basics

Make sure you have the correct spelling of the agent's name; make sure you know whether this person is a male or a female; and address him as you would address anyone you don't know in a business letter.

I have received query letters addressed to Ms. Evan Marshall, Miss Eva Marshall, and Mr. Evan Marshal. I admit that I still read the letter; but there are many other agents who won't. Please don't call me Evan unless you really know me on a first-name basis, and I will afford you the same courtesy. Mr. Marshall will do fine for now. There's an old convention in publishing of using a person's entire name: Dear Evan Marshall. I suppose there's nothing wrong with it. I find it precious and pretentious.

The Essential Power Elements

In your query letter, be sure to use the Essential Power Elements: important components that ensure the best possible presentation. For that's exactly what this is: a marketing presentation, and your first impression to boot.

Before I present the Essential Power Elements, here's a basic and important rule: Keep your query letter to one page. Multipage query letters, like multipage résumés, are often tossed out, as unfair as that may be.

Here are the Essential Power Elements. Use them whenever you approach an agent or editor about a novel—at any time in your career—and you can't go wrong.

The Referral

You may not have this helpful element, but if you do, it goes first. It's just what it sounds like: If another writer the agent represents has referred you to his or her agent, say so. Ideally, the name of the person who has referred you starts the letter.

> **HELPFUL HINT:** Here's a sneaky way to get a referral. Keep your eyes open for a book signing in your area featuring an author who writes the kind of book you're writing or have written. Call the store ahead of time and find out when the signing will be over. On the day of the signing, arrive about ten minutes before the end, then be sure you're one of the last people—if not the last person—to buy one of the author's books and ask him to sign it. Before he starts packing up to leave, engage him in a brief conversation about his novel, then mention that you're at work on (or have completed) a novel in the same genre. You're ready to start showing it, and would he mind if you sent it to his agent and/or editor and mentioned his name? Chances are good he'll say yes.

The Hook

This is your angle, your novel's "high concept." Some people call it the sound byte. Many novelists simply adapt their pitch (see page 66). The hook is usually only a short paragraph, but it's the most important part of the query letter because it's the first thing the recipient will read, and it sums up your story in a way that will make it extremely easy for the reader to either plunk your letter onto the rejection-slip pile or read on with interest. I don't have to tell you which result you're after.

The Stats

In the next paragraph, tell the reader your novel's title, its genre, and its word count (just multiply the number of manuscript pages by 250 and round to the nearest ten thousand—this is close enough). In this paragraph you may also elaborate a little on the hook presented in the first paragraph.

HELPFUL HINT: Is your novel's word length in the appropriate range for its genre? At my agency we receive many query letters about novels that are clearly too long or too short for their genres. Find out appropriate word length through your research, publishers' tip sheets (guidelines), or simply by calculating the word length of books like yours. One easy method of doing this is to use the following formula: number of book pages × number of lines on a *full* page × 9 = number of words.

The Meat

Here's where you describe—in a not-overly-long paragraph—your story. Make it as interesting as you can, and don't try to tell the whole story. Make it more of a setup, the kind of thing you might read on the back of a paperback book, except that you'll leave out any words of praise for your own work—a definite red flag that signals "Amateur!"

You

In this paragraph you talk about yourself, but only in ways relevant to your novel. If your occupation or experience make you especially qualified to have written this novel, explain why. List also any previous writing credits, and any relevant organizations or writers' groups you belong to.

> **HELPFUL HINT:** For some inexplicable reason, writers often include in their query letters the titles of their published books, but not the names of the publishers, even when these are highly respected companies. Be sure to tell the agent or editor not only what you've written but exactly who published it.

The Audience

Now tell the agent or editor who your novel will appeal to. You might say that it will appeal to fans of certain genres of fiction, or that it will appeal to fans of certain authors who write similar books. (But don't say you write just as well as, or better than, a published writer.)

The Closer

Finish up with something along the lines of *Thank you for your consideration. I look forward to your response*, then a nice businesslike *Sincerely* or *Very truly yours*, and you've got a great query letter . . . once you've read it and reread it until it's your best writing and letter perfect.

The Format

Type your query letter, single-spaced, with 1″ margins, on either your letterhead (unless it says *Writer* or *Author* on it, in which case you should have your letterhead redone without it, since agents and editors consider it amateurish) or a sheet of plain white paper with your address and telephone number typed beneath your name at the bottom. Your query letter should never be handwritten.

Enclose with your query letter a stamped, self-addressed No. 10 business-size envelope (SASE), folded in thirds, for the agent's reply. Send the query and SASE by first class mail.

> **HELPFUL HINT:** Do not send your query letter by Certified Mail—Return Receipt Requested, FedEx, Express Mail, or any other method that requires a signature. If the agent or her assistant is not in the office when the letter arrives, someone will probably have to go to the post office or make special arrangements to get it. Most agents won't bother, or if they do, they'll be so annoyed to find a query letter in that envelope rather than a check that they'll probably turn you down just out of spite! Good old First Class Mail works just fine.

Use the Marshall Planner: The Perfect Query Letter on page 111 to customize your own query. You'll find sample query letters in Appendix A.

To "E" or Not to "E"

Should you send a query letter by e-mail? That depends. First, check the directories on page 131 to see if the agent you want to approach has any policy about e-queries. Some don't mind them; others state explicitly that they don't want them. If the directories make no mention of e-mail queries, call the agent's office and simply ask.

If an e-query is acceptable, follow all of the rules above; don't suddenly get casual simply because e-mail is, for the most part, a more casual medium than old-fashioned letters on paper. What you do have in an e-mail query that you don't in a paper query is the *SUBJECT* line. Make it clear here that you are not selling cheap Viagra or mortgages; use the word *Query*. It doesn't hurt to say what you're querying about: *Query about a thriller*, or *Query about a romance novel*.

Very often I receive e-queries whose *TO:* or *CC:* line contains a seemingly endless list of agencies' e-mail addresses. These e-mails make me feel as if the writer didn't do his homework and is querying every agent whose e-mail address he can find, hoping one of them will be appropriate for the work in question. And this is basically what is happening. I quickly lose interest in these queries. If you are querying a number of agents, be smart: send the queries separately. (Don't use the *BCC:* option, because if you do the *TO:* line won't contain each individual agent's name.)

Something else that turns many agents off in this age of the computer virus is e-mail attachments. At my agency we make it a standard practice not to open them. If you have followed my advice and sent only a query letter, there shouldn't be anything to attach. But those of you who may still feel something additional is necessary—(a résumé? a credit list? your favorite recipe?) should keep this aversion to attachments in mind.

Most likely you'll get a faster response to an e-query than you will to a paper one, but don't get discouraged if your e-mail isn't answered instantly. Agents and other busy people sometimes put off dealing with their e-mail. Despite your best efforts, your query may get deleted. If you receive no response, don't send it again; figure the agent wasn't interested.

What's my query preference? I still prefer the old-fashioned paper ones. Maybe it's because I'm used to seeing how people express themselves on paper and like this medium as a way of getting acquainted. I believe paper queries are the smarter option for you, too, since it's much harder for a conscientious agent to justify discarding a self-addressed stamped envelope than it is to justify pressing DELETE.

The Art of the Synopsis

Many new writers think that when their manuscripts are finished, their work is done. Wrong! Nowadays agents and editors are likely to ask to see a synopsis as well as your manuscript. As a marketing tool, the synopsis is even more important than the query letter—though if your query letter isn't just right, you won't reach the synopsis stage at all.

Too often at my agency I hear something to the effect of, "Why should I have to write a synopsis of my novel? I've already written the novel!" Or, "By the time I finish the synopsis, I could have half the novel written!"

Unfortunately, the synopsis is a necessary tool you're going to have to learn to master if you want to make it as a novelist. It's something agents need; very often, in response to a query letter, they will ask to see a synopsis and the first three chapters of your novel, or they may ask to see the synopsis alone. Everyone works differently.

Editors, too, need a synopsis. They often request that a writer or agent include one *with* the manuscript. Why? Editors are extremely overworked and must plow through mountains of material. A simple way to find out whether a novel is worth spending a lot of time on is to read the sample chapters, and if the writing is appealing, read the synopsis to see if the writer also knows how to plot a good story. Those are the two factors agents and editors look for in their hunt for new talent: good writing and good storytelling. (For plotting advice, see *The Marshall Plan for Novel Writing* and *The Marshall Plan Workbook*.)

The synopsis will have other uses as well. Once you've sold your novel, the synopsis will bounce around your publisher, getting photocopied by various departments that need it for different reasons. The sales department needs it to write catalog copy. The copy chief needs it, perhaps along with the manuscript, to either write cover or jacket copy or assign the job to a freelancer. The publicity and promotion departments will need it to write sales collateral and press releases, and to pitch your novel to the media effectively.

Once you've made your first sale, you'll be glad you know how to write a bang-up synopsis, because then you'll be able to land a contract on a synopsis and sample chapters, or on a synopsis alone. Cool!

But before you make that first sale, the synopsis is your second foot in the door, often the material read first in the decision as to whether to pursue your book further.

> **HELPFUL HINT:** Got screenwriting aspirations? Then that's one more reason to learn the art of the synopsis. A great synopsis is virtually the same as a film treatment. Master this skill and you'll be one step closer to Hollywood!

Synopsis Basics

So what, exactly, *is* a synopsis? It's a summary of your novel, written in a way that conveys the excitement of the novel itself. Before we get into how to do that, here are some basic things you should know about setting up your synopsis.

The format of your synopsis is similar to that of your actual manuscript. Follow the guidelines for manuscript preparation starting on page 106, except that your slugline should look like this:

Marshall/TOASTING TINA/Synopsis   46

Your synopsis doesn't need a title page, but you should set up its first page as follows:

Against the top and left margins, type *single-spaced* your real name, mailing address, telephone number, and e-mail address.

Against the top and right margins, type your novel's genre (for example, mystery, romance, Westerns; see *The Marshall Plan for Novel Writing* or *The Marshall Plan Workbook* for complete genre lists). Under that, type your word count, rounded to the nearest 10,000. And under that, type the word *Synopsis*.

Double-space twice from the bottom of all this text and type your novel's title, centered and in all capital letters. Double-space once and type *by*, double-space again, and type your name (or pseudonym if you're using one).

Double-space again and, indenting the first paragraph, start the text of your synopsis. Double-space all the rest.

The synopsis is always written in the *present* tense (known as the historical present tense).

In the synopsis, you tell your *whole* story. You do not— even in the case of a mystery—leave out the solution in an attempt to induce an agent or editor to request the manuscript. Nor do you pick up where your sample chapters leave off. As mentioned above, your synopsis is your novel, your *entire* novel, in miniature.

There's no hard-and-fast rule about how long a synopsis should be, but most agents and editors agree that a too-long synopsis defeats its own purpose. Some agents and editors request extremely short synopses, which aren't really synopses at all, but more like jacket or cover copy, or what Hollywood calls "coverage." If such a thing is specifically requested, then you should of course comply. But for the most part a synopsis is a longer piece of work. As a rule, I like to aim for a page of synopsis for every twenty-five pages of manuscript. This would mean a four hundred-page manuscript gets a synopsis of about sixteen pages. But this rule is often broken, depending on the novel itself. A mystery, for example, may require a longer synopsis because of the level of detail that must be presented. Eventually you'll find yourself allowing your synopses to seek their own length, and that they'll almost always come out about right.

To achieve such conciseness, you must write as clean and tight as you know how. Don't do what many writers do and try to keep boiling down your actual novel again and again until it's short enough. First of all, this is a waste of your precious time. Second, these boil-downs usually read very strangely.

Instead, learn to write in a synoptic style—read a section or chapter of your novel and simply retell it, as you might describe a great book or movie to a friend.

Leaving out unnecessary adverbs and adjectives, focus on your story's essential points. Much must be left out, such as inconsequential specifics of a particular incident.

Don't write:

> At work, Elizabeth searches for Peter all over the office and finally finds him in the supply room, where she tells him she resents the remarks he made about her in the staff meeting.

Write:

> At work, Elizabeth confronts Peter about his remarks at the staff meeting.

That's all we need to know at this point.

Actual dialogue from your novel is rarely needed, though a few chosen lines can be effective. Remember, overall, that whereas in a novel you should *show* rather than *tell*, in a synopsis you *should* tell. Here it's okay simply to write *Yvette is furious*, though you would not write that in your novel (see Tip 19 on page 20); you would *show* us how Yvette's anger manifests itself.

Write your synopsis as one unified narrative. Don't divide

it into sections or chapters. Use paragraphing and short transitions to signify these breaks: *The next morning. . . . But when he arrives at the fair. . . . Meanwhile, in the deserted warehouse. . . . Across town, in a small park. . . .*

If you've read other writing books, you're probably wondering about character sketches. Again, if an agent or editor specifically requests them, you'd better write them. Otherwise, my advice is to omit them. I hate character sketches. At the beginning of the synopsis, where one finds them, they are meaningless because we are learning about people outside the context of a story. I much prefer a brief description of the character when he or she is introduced in the synopsis:

> . . . Gilbert drives to the laboratory and discovers that a woman named REBECCA MURRAY has gotten there first. Rebecca, a striking redhead in her early twenties, is outraged, believing that Gilbert has been sent to supervise her. She screams at him to get out. . . .

You no doubt noticed that Rebecca's name is in all capital letters. Use this technique, borrowed from film treatments, whenever you introduce a character. It makes keeping track of your story people a bit easier for the reader.

Professional novelists know how to put together a synopsis that makes agents and editors sit up and take notice—and ask for the manuscript. Here are the tricks they use.

The Hook

To create an arresting hook for your synopsis, start with your story's lead character and the crisis that has befallen him—

the crisis that begins the story. Then explain what your lead must do in order to remedy the crisis; in other words, what is his story goal? For example:

> RHONDA STERN has always considered herself immune to the danger and unpleasantness of the outside world, quietly creating tapestries in the house she occupies alone on lush, secluded Bainbridge Island, Washington. But the world intrudes in a horrible way when one morning a desperate criminal breaks into Rhonda's home and takes her hostage, threatening to kill her if she doesn't help him get off the island. Now Rhonda must fight to save her life while at the same time trying not to help a man she knows is guilty of murder.

HELPFUL HINT: Try starting your hook paragraph with a question. *What would you do if a desperate criminal broke into your home and took you hostage?* A provocative question like this not only grabs the reader's attention but immediately throws him into the situation—a desirable effect.

The Back-Up

Right after your hook paragraph, back up a little to give some further background that makes the situation clearer. This is where you should also make sure you've covered the basics: your lead's age, occupation, marital status (if you haven't already given us this information in the hook); the time (past—if so, when?—present, or future); and the place.

> Rhonda, a blonde, ethereally beautiful 24-
> year-old, has heard about a string of murders
> on the island, but the authorities believe the killer
> has already escaped to the mainland. But he's
> here, in her house, and now Rhonda finds herself
> wishing she hadn't asked her husband to
> move out only two weeks ago.

The Meat

Now move on to the action of your story. Give us not only the things that happen to make up your plot but also—and I can't stress this enough—*how your lead character feels about them or is affected by them.*

So many synopses are dull because the author has left out the emotional component. Remember that people read novels primarily to be moved emotionally; they want to live the story through the lead. The only way they can do that is to know how the lead feels.

In other words, emotions and feelings *are* plot; they are as important as the things that happen.

> The intruder, who introduces himself as
> RYDER GANNON, barricades himself
> and Rhonda in her workroom, allowing her
> to leave only to get him some food. He is
> limping and she soon discovers why: he has

an ugly gash in his upper thigh—the work,
he says, of a neighbor's vicious dog. He's
bleeding profusely. He tells Rhonda to
bring him some rags to wrap around the
wound, and as she watches him her heart
goes out to him, in spite of what she believes
he's done, for under his matted blond hair
and mud-smeared face he is little more than
a boy, eighteen perhaps. She finds herself
helping him, and as he watches her, he tells
her he didn't really kill those people,
though he knows who did. . . .

Dynamics

Words are precious in the synopsis, so pick the best ones you
can! Use strong action words, and keep the action crisp,
clean, and clear.

Rhonda says she doesn't believe him, that if
he's capable of holding her hostage in her
own house, he's capable of the things the police
say he did. Suddenly furious, Ryder slaps
Rhonda so hard she's thrown onto her back.
She begins to cry, begging him to just get
out and leave her alone.

Think Miniature

Very often in a novel, there are secrets and other information
that must at some point be revealed. For some reason,
many writers believe that in a synopsis they must reveal all
of this information right up front. Not so. In your synop-

sis, reveal secrets and other surprising information in exactly the same spots where you have done so (or intend to do so) in the novel itself.

Stay Out of It

Don't let your scaffolding show. By this I mean don't use devices that suggest the mechanical aspects of your story. This is another reason you shouldn't run character sketches at the beginning of the synopsis, or use headings within the synopsis such as *Background* or *Setting*. Work these elements smoothly into the story; give us background when it's necessary for the reader to understand something.

Don't refer to your novel's structural underpinnings. Don't write: *In a flashback, Rhonda remembers an episode with DENIS during their honeymoon.* Just write: *During her and DENIS's honeymoon, Rhonda. . . .* Don't write: *At the story's climax. . . .* And don't review your own work: *In a poignant encounter, Rhonda. . . .*

Pace It Right

As you near the end of your story, indicate its quickened pace by using shorter paragraphs that give a speeded-up, staccato effect.

Rhonda stands at the edge of the bridge, her gaze locked on Ryder as he slips deeper into the water.

At the other end of the bridge, Denis cries out

to her, begging her to believe he's not the killer.

Rhonda makes her decision. . . .

Maximum Drama

This is your novel in miniature, and you want to leave the reader of your synopsis with the same great feeling he'll have after reading your book. The way to do that is to slow down a little at the novel's end, after the story has resolved itself and you're in the Wrap-Up, and really bear down on the emotional elements. These are what produce that goose-bumps-at-the-back-of-the-neck feeling when we finish a wonderful novel. Go into more detail here; give us a line of dialogue if that's appropriate.

> Rhonda cradles Ryder in her arms and whispers that he'll be all right. In the distance they hear the wail of sirens. He smiles up at her and tells her it took a while for him to convince her of his innocence, but he's glad he didn't give up.
> "Neither am I," she murmurs, tenderly kissing his forehead. "Neither am I."

HELPFUL HINT: Very often, the last actual line or short paragraph of the novel itself makes a perfect ending for the synopsis as well. Just remember to change the past tense to the present tense. The paragraph above could have come from a novel:

"Neither am I," she murmured, tenderly kissing his forehead. "Neither am I."

Polish It

The editing of your synopsis is, in a way, more important than the editing of your book—though I would never tell you it's okay to do less than your best work on either.

Because a synopsis is briefer than a novel, errors stand out more clearly. Make yours as close to perfect as you can, even if that means several rounds of editing. Check for misspelled words, awkward sentence structure, confusing writing, grammatical errors, and typographical errors. Be consistent in referring to your characters: don't write *Ryder* in one place and *Gannon* in another. Stick with one name for each character to avoid confusion.

> **HELPFUL HINT:** Give the synopsis to someone else to read for typos, misspellings, and logical flaws. Sometimes when we're so close to something we miss errors no matter how many times our eyes pass over them. If you decide to proof your synopsis yourself, print it out; don't proof it on your computer monitor. Published authors agree that, for some reason, it's easy to miss mistakes on the screen.

Use the Marshall Planner: The Perfect Synopsis on page 112 to customize your synopsis. You'll find sample synopses in Appendix C.

The Short Synopsis

There is a general trend these days toward shorter synopses. Some agents and editors now request synopses of 1,500 words (about six manuscript pages). Others like three pages, and still others ask for only one! Some complicate matters by asking for a one-page synopsis with your query letter; then, if they like what they see, they ask to see a longer synopsis and sample chapters.

This means two things: (1) You need to learn to write the short synopsis, and (2) you must be ready to adjust the length of your short synopsis according to the specific requirements of the person to whom you're submitting.

Here are some tips for writing the short synopsis:

- Use the present (historical present) tense, as for the long synopsis.
- Lead off with a strong hook sentence—anything that will grab the attention of your reader. Hint: Look to your pitch for ideas. A "what if" is sometimes an intriguing way to begin.
- Paragraph only for broad transitions in your story.
- Use no dialogue.
- Quickly introduce your lead, the opposition, the romantic interest, and any other important characters, while setting up the story in terms of place and time.
- Quickly state the conflict between your lead and the opposition; then state the lead's story goal.
- Stick to the high points of your lead's main story line.
- Do not include any subplots.
- Move smoothly from one event to another; avoid the choppiness often seen in beginners' short synopses— a result of having whittled down a longer synopsis without regard for smoothness of reading.

- Use powerful verbs and few if any adverbs and adjectives.
- Tell the entire story.

You'll find a sample short synopsis in Appendix D.

Make it your business to master the synopsis. Don't be one of those writers who says, "I just can't write a synopsis." They're usually the writers who get the poorer deals or no deal at all.

The synopsis is as necessary a tool for a novelist as, say, the preliminary study is for many painters. Once you get the technique down, you'll probably even find writing the synopsis fun.

The Art of the Cover Letter

If you follow the advice above and write a knockout query letter, chances are good that one or more agents will agree to look at your work. In this case you will receive in your SASE not a "no, thank you" letter or rejection slip, but an "I would be happy to read your novel" letter. When this happens, you're going to want to be ready to send your manuscript and/or a synopsis of your novel, depending on what the agent requests.

But it's not enough to just throw your manuscript into an envelope and mail it off. You now need a cover letter to accompany your manuscript and reintroduce yourself to the agent—who, believe it or not, may have no recollection of you or your query.

So do some reminding. Like the query letter, the cover letter should be polished to perfection.

HELPFUL HINT: A lot of writers have no problem writing a synopsis; the problem is that they don't how to plot! Here, in a nutshell, are some tips for creating a solidly plotted novel:

Once you have decided on your novel's genre, select a lead appropriate to this genre: man, woman, teen, child.

Devise a genre-appropriate crisis for your lead that will turn her life upside down and make her want to set her life right again by gaining possession of something or relief from something. This desire is your lead's story goal.

Taking cues and clues from the type of lead you've chosen and the kind of crisis she faces, flesh out your lead and decide on other characters who would logically be part of your lead's world. The most important characters to define are the opposition, the confidant and, if appropriate to your genre, the romantic involvement.

Set your lead in action, setting small goals toward achieving the larger story goal. Write in action sections, in which your lead tries to achieve a section goal, is hindered by another character or characters (or circumstances), and then fails to achieve this section goal. This failure causes her to set a new goal, which will be the subject of the next action section.

If your lead experiences a major or especially upsetting failure—or needs time to analyze in depth what

continued

has just taken place—use a reaction section to show her response. In this section, show your lead's emotional and then rational reactions to the failure she's just experienced; then have her set a goal for her next section. Otherwise simply go on to another action section.

In your novel's beginning (the first quarter of the manuscript), introduce all major characters and present all background information as you string together your action and reaction sections. Introduce a second, subordinate goal for your lead, as well as story lines involving other characters. The only character whose action sections may end with success rather than failure is the opposition. If you're new to plotting, try to keep your story lines separate— even the lead's main story line from his or her subordinate story line.

At the end of your novel's beginning, introduce an especially bad or shocking surprise (Surprise No. 1) that raises the stakes for your lead and/or sends the story in a new direction.

In your novel's middle (which constitutes half the manuscript's length), continue stringing together action and reaction sections. Alternate sections involving your lead with sections involving other characters' story lines. To weave story lines, present an action section ending with one character's failure, switch to another character's action section ending with that character's failure, then switch back to the previous (or another) character in either a new action section or, if appropriate, a reaction section.

Keep raising the stakes, ruling out options, making it look less and less likely that your lead will achieve the story goal.

In the very center of your manuscript, end an action section for your lead with Surprise No. 2, another shocking revelation or development that spins the story off in a new direction or makes things much worse for your lead. At the end of your novel's middle (three-quarters of the way through your manuscript), use the same technique as above to insert Surprise No. 3.

Your novel's end (the last quarter of your manuscript) is where your story heats up as the lead desperately tries to achieve the story goal with not much time and few options left. Tie off subordinate story lines and loose ends; all but the pursuit of the story goal—and the romantic story line, if you have one—should be resolved.

Now devise an action section called the Worst Failure, featuring your lead against the opposition. End this section with the worst failure yet. Follow with a reaction section called the Point of Hopelessness, in which your lead reacts to this failure so devastating that achieving the story goal now appears hopeless. Follow this with an action section called the Saving Act, in which your lead, drawing on some special

continued

talent or revelation, performs an act that reverses the entire situation and vanquishes the opposition. Story goal achieved!

Finish with a brief wrap-up showing life turned right side up again for your lead. Last of all, resolve the romantic story line.

Voilà!

Cover Letter Basics

First of all, match your salutation to that of the agent's letter. If he addresses you by your first name, it's all right for you to do the same with him. If he addresses you as a Mr. or Ms., do the same back.

Next, express your appreciation of the agent's willingness to read your work. Be sure to mention that he *requested* that you send it.

If you originally met this agent at a writers conference, at a convention, at a party, or at the health club, remind him of this. If your original contact was by means of a referral or recommendation, mention it.

State once again the title of your novel, its genre, and its word count. Then give a shortened version of "The Meat" (see page 94), just as a reminder of what the book is about. Remember that agents receive hundreds and hundreds of letters, and will be grateful rather than insulted to be reminded about what they have asked to see.

Remind the agent of anything else pertinent to your submission—special relevant experience you've had, previous writing credits, organizations you belong to.

Then just say something like, "I look forward to your response" and leave it at that.

Use the Marshall Planner: The Perfect Cover Letter on page 114 to create a customized cover letter. You'll find a sample cover letter in Appendix B.

CHAPTER 12

Your Manuscript: Rules for Setting It Up Exactly Right

Your novel is completed. Every word is the way you want it, but the manuscript itself is a mess—full of cross-outs, pages taped and stapled together, scribbled additions that flow onto the backs of pages. Now's the time to whip the manuscript into shape, to make it conform to the format that professional novelists use—and that agents and editors are used to seeing. It's all quite simple.

Use white 8½″ × 11″ paper. Most writers present their final manuscripts on 20-pound copier-type paper. For more durability and a more luxurious feel, use 20-pound paper with 25 percent cotton fiber (rag) content. Do not use onion skin, erasable, or colored paper.

Type on one side of the page only.

Your left, right, and bottom margins should be set at 1¼″, your top margin at ½″.

All text (except for a few lines on your title page, which I'll talk about below) should be double-spaced.

Number your manuscript pages consecutively (not by chapter), beginning with the first page after the title page (the title page is not numbered); place the page number in the upper-right corner of the page, against the right and top margins. Do not use the word *Page* before the number, enclose it in hyphens, or put a period after it. Just put the number.

Against the upper and left margins of every page except the title page, you'll create a "slugline," which consists of your last name in upper- and lowercase letters, followed by a slash, followed by your novel's title in all capital letters. Your computer's word-processing program is likely to have a header feature that can automatically place this slugline on all pages for you. Thus, the top of every page of your manuscript except the title page will look like this:

Marshall/TOASTING TINA   365

On every page of your manuscript except the title page and the first pages of chapters—in other words, on your all-text pages—the first text line should be ¾" below the slugline and page number.

Set your computer to justify (make even) your left margin only. Leave the right margin uneven, or "ragged," as we say in publishing.

Don't break and hyphenate words at the ends of lines. Doing so only makes the job of your publisher's production department more difficult.

Use a good-quality laser or inkjet printer. No dot matrix, the bane of agents' and editors' existence—and probably part of the reason most of us wear glasses!

Use a simple font such as Courier (12-point) or Times New Roman (12-point) or Arial (12-point). Publishing people used to carry on about restricting the font to Courier, but the fact is that many published novelists now use these other simple fonts. The key is to be consistent. Use one font and stick to it throughout your manuscript. Type should be black only; never use any other color.

Another old rule was that italics were to be indicated by underlining, but many novelists now use actual italics in their manuscripts. It's up to you; again, just be consistent. Do not use boldface.

Indent every paragraph half an inch. Do not leave any extra space between paragraphs. To indicate a space break between sections, leave a blank line by pressing Enter twice. If the break falls at the beginning or end of a page, indicate the break with one centered asterisk.

To start a new chapter, type *Chapter One* (or whatever the number is) a third of the way down the page, or at about 3.7 inches. Most word-processing programs will tell you how far down the page you are. Then leave a blank line (press Enter twice) and start your text, indented, on the next line.

When you get to the end of your manuscript, just stop. Do not type *The End* or *Finis* or # or anything else. If it's not clear from your text that this is the end of the book, you've got a problem.

After a period, type two spaces if you are using Courier, one space if you are using Times New Roman, Arial, Helvetica, or another proportional font.

Indicate a dash by typing two hyphens together, with no space between the hyphens and the words to the left and right. Some people like to set their word processing programs to automatically turn these two hyphens into actual em dashes, as they are called. This is fine.

Place commas inside quotation marks for dialogue: *"I'm leaving," Edward said.*

Type an ellipsis as three periods with one space before and after each one, as follows: *Oh, what I could do for your career . . .*

If your ellipsis follows a period at the end of a sentence, type it like this: *Well, I didn't think Margery was there that night.* . . . Then leave one space and start your new sentence, as I've just done.

Use single quotation marks only to indicate quotation marks within quotation marks, like so: "*When I asked him what he was doing, he said, 'Mind your own business!'* "

Don't bind the pages of your manuscript in any way. Just place the pages loose in a manuscript box (you can buy these at most office-supply stores) or an empty computer paper box.

> **HELPFUL HINT:** Nobody knows everything about grammar, punctuation, and style. Keep a good dictionary and style manual next to your computer at all times, and don't be lazy about checking something you're unsure about. Most publishers follow *Merriam-Webster's Collegiate Dictionary* (Springfield, MA: Merriam-Webster, Inc., 10th ed.) and either *The Chicago Manual of Style* (Chicago: The University of Chicago Press, 14th ed.) or *Words Into Type*, Skillin, Marjorie E., and Gay, Robert M. (Englewood Cliffs, NJ: Prentice-Hall, Inc., 3rd ed.)

The Title Page

Create a simple title page for your manuscript. As mentioned above, the title page is never numbered.

In the upper-left corner of the page, against the left and

upper margins, type single-spaced your real name; under that, your city, state, and zip code; under that, your telephone number; and under that, your e-mail address. Do not add your Social Security Number or anything about copyright or the rights you're offering—two signs of the amateur. In the upper-right corner of the page, type the manuscript's word count, determined by multiplying the number of manuscript pages by 250 and rounding to the nearest 10,000—for example: 120,000 Words. Centered halfway down the page, and double-spaced, type your novel's title in all capital letters, type *by* on the next line, and type your name (or pseudonym if you're using one) on the next line.

That's really all there is to it. If I haven't mentioned it here, don't do it. I would give you a list of manuscript don'ts except that I've seen so many in my years as an editor and agent that the list would take pages and pages: manuscripts bound with ribbon, sprinkled with perfume, smeared with blood (this for a vampire novel—I'm serious!), printed to look like actual books, shrink-wrapped . . . you get the idea.

If you follow these guidelines, your manuscript will be in the form agents and editors are used to, and will signal to them that you are a professional. Sometimes manuscripts are rejected simply because of how they look. Why have a strike against you before you've even begun?

Marshall Planner: The Perfect Query Letter

	Date	**TIP:** **Query letter should** **be single–spaced** **and no longer** **than one page.**
Mr./Ms.	**Agent or Editor's Name**	
	Title (If an Editor)	
	Company	
	Address	
	City, State, Zip	
Dear Mr./Ms. :	**Salutation**	**WRITING COACH**
		REFERRAL; THE HOOK **(high concept)**
		THE STATS: **Title, genre, words;** **more Hook**
		THE MEAT: **Briefly describe** **story setup**
		THE AUDIENCE: **Fans of certain genre** **or author (s)**
		YOU: **Relevant background;** **credits; memberships**
May I send you the manuscript of ?		**THE REQUEST**
Sincerely,		
	Your Signature	
	Your Name	
	E-mail Address	
	Address	
	City, State, Zip	

Marshall Planner: The Perfect Synopsis

	Your Name	Genre	
	Address		,000 Words
	City, State, Zip		Word count Synopsis
	Telephone Number		to the
	E-mail Address		nearest
			10,000

TIP:
Aim for 1 page of synopsis per 25 pages of manuscript.

	Title

by

	Pseudonym, if using one, or name

WRITING COACH

THE HOOK:
Lead, crisis, story goal

THE BACKUP:
Background; lead's stats, time, and place

THE MEAT:
Action of story

(TIP: Include not just events but also characters' motivations, reactions, emotions)

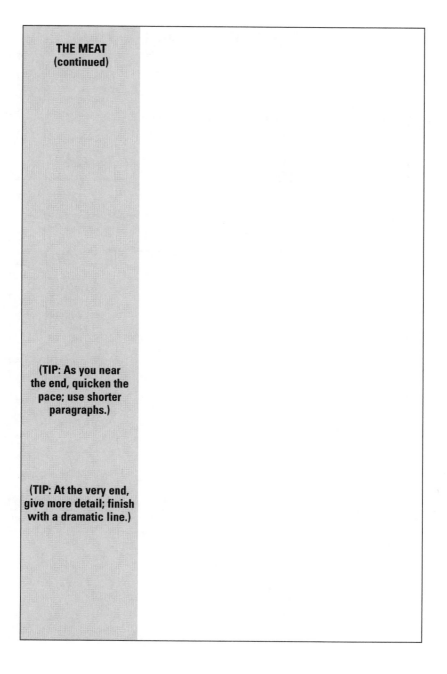

THE MEAT
(continued)

(TIP: As you near the end, quicken the pace; use shorter paragraphs.)

(TIP: At the very end, give more detail; finish with a dramatic line.)

Marshall Planner: The Perfect Cover Letter

		TIP: Cover letter should be single–spaced and no longer than one page.
	Date	
Mr./Ms.	Agent or Editor's Name	
	Title (If an Editor)	
	Company	**WRITING COACH**
	Address	
	City, State, Zip	
Dear :		**SALUTATION:** Match to agent's or editor's letter
Thank you for agreeing to read my manuscipt, [TITLE].		**THANKS**
		REMINDER: How you first made contact with the agent or editor
		THE STATS & THE MEAT: Reminder of genre, word count, what book is about (adapt pitch; see page 66)
		YOU: Reminder of relevant background and credentials
I look forward to your response.		**THE CLOSING**
Sincerely,		
	Your Signature	
	Your Name	
	Address	
	City, State, Zip	

Section II

THE PITCH

CHAPTER 13

Your Submission Campaign

Your novel is completed and all of your auxiliary materials—
query letter, synopsis, short synopsis, cover letter—are
ready. Now what do you do?

You *don't* start sending things out helter-skelter, hoping
something will hit the target. You take a thoughtful, intelli-
gent, businesslike approach to submission. You plan a
campaign.

A Multitiered Approach

I always recommend a multitiered approach: querying agents,
querying editors, meeting agents, and meeting editors. If
you've ever submitted anything before, you know why I recommend this approach. Most agents and editors take a
long time to reply to writers' queries, not because they're mean
or don't care, but because in the grand scheme of things,
material from people you don't already represent or publish
is not as important as material from people you do. A wait
of several months up to a year is not uncommon. If you queried
one agent at a time, one editor at a time, you could be in
your dotage by the time you got an answer. Agents know how

slow editors can be. That's why we often make simultaneous submissions.

Which agents and editors do you query? Which ones do you try to meet, and how?

In chapter fifteen, I talk about researching agents to find the ones right for you and your work. In chapter fourteen, I discuss submitting directly to editors, since (despite what you hear) many still accept queries and often ask to see manuscripts in response to these queries.

Make a number of copies of the Marshall Planner: Submission Log on page 156 and, based on your research, write down the names, addresses, telephone numbers, and, if they're listed, the e-mail addresses of the agents and editors you think will have an interest in your novel.

Immediately query all of these agents and editors, following the guidelines in chapter ten. On the Marshall Planner: Submission Log, keep a record of exactly what you send to whom and when you send it. Number the entries. If positive responses come in, record those, too: *Requested synopsis and first three chapters*, or *Requested complete manuscript*, or whatever the case may be. Then, in the extreme-right column, write the number of the next blank on your Marshall Planner: Submission Log. There you'll fill in the agent's or editor's address and contact information again, and record what you're sending this time. Negative responses, of course, end there, though you should make a note about the response: *Not accepting new clients*, or *Not enthusiastic*, or maybe just *Printed rejection slip*. Or you might simply want to write *See letter*. Keep all correspondence you receive from agents and editors in a file or folder with your Marshall Planner: Submission Log.

As you're querying and acting on positive responses, keep your eyes out for new names. You might read about an interesting deal in *Publishers Weekly* or online in *Publishers Lunch* (see page 134). You might read a book like yours and see an acknowledgment to an agent or editor not on your list. If so, jot down this person's name, consult one of the directories on page 131, and query! In other words, always keep your material moving. Most importantly, do not allow negative responses to immobilize you.

Don't Take It Personally

You've got to develop a rhinoceros hide in this business. Never forget that an agent's or editor's opinion is just that—his or her opinion—and nothing more. Also keep in mind that most agents and editors do not give reasons for turning material down; they don't have time, and even if they did, they don't want to get into a dialogue or critique—unless they see promise and want to encourage you. Therefore, you'll often get those blasted one-size-fits-all rejection slips that tell you nothing at all.

Sometimes the reasons behind these maddening sheets of paper have nothing to do with your material. An agent or editor may not be accepting unpublished writers but does not want to say so. He may not be accepting new clients at all unless they are exceptional, but does not want to say so because then submissions would drop off—a bad situation for an agent. He may already have a novel signed up that is similar to yours. The point is, it doesn't matter why someone rejects you; make a note of it and move on, knowing that rejection is an inevitable part of the process.

Keep It Moving

While you're querying, following up on positive responses, and watching constantly for new agent or editor names, keep an eye on directories, newsletters, and Web sites such as Shaw Guides (www.shawguides.com) for conferences you feel are worth attending. You may not be able to cross the country to attend a national convention in your genre, but there's really no excuse for not showing up at a local conference—even a general writers conference—especially if agents who handle your kind of writing will be attending.

In chapter ten, I discuss the etiquette of meeting with agents and editors at conferences. When you do make contact in this way, be sure to ask the all-important question: "May I send you my manuscript?" If the answer is yes, record that agent's or editor's contact information on your Marshall Planner: Submission Log as soon as you get home, then get that material into the mail, making certain to record the details—what you're sending and when you're sending it.

And so it goes. Never hold back from submitting to a new name you've discovered; there's no limit to the number of queries you can have out at the same time. If an agent or editor requests exclusivity, follow the guidelines on page 72 to handle the situation correctly.

The key is to keep your material on submission, and to always be on the lookout for new names. Things change over time. Editors change jobs, or new ones appear. The same goes for agents. Publishing is such a merry-go-round that sometimes it seems its entire personnel profile can change over the course of a single year.

Oh, there's one more thing you need to do while you're keeping all the submission balls in the air: Keep writing. Why?

HELPFUL HINT: Very often agents are open to new clients but must be extremely selective because they already have full client lists. Try targeting newer agents at large agencies. You may read (for example, in the People section of *Publishers Weekly*) that an editor has become an agent, or that an assistant at a literary agency has been promoted to full agent. If you have any reason to believe this person might be right for your novel, query him immediately. Another trick is simply to call the switchboards of large agencies and ask if there are any new agents. Very often the receptionist will tell you their names and specialties.

First and foremost, because you're a writer, and that's what writers do. On a more practical level, an agent or editor might decline your current project but ask to see something else. You'll want to have that "something else" ready as soon as possible.

Follow these guidelines and eventually you'll find yourself on the receiving end of a string of positive responses from an agent or editor who understands and appreciates what you're doing. He's out there somewhere, and wants to meet you as badly as you want to meet him. Don't give up. That person could be the next one on your list.

CHAPTER 14

Yes, It Is Okay to Approach Editors (Sometimes): How to Do It Right

In spite of all I've said about publishers accepting agented sub-missions only, and about what an agent can do for a writer, there are still many instances in which you don't necessarily need an agent.

Note that if you do approach publishers directly, you will probably still need a query letter (see the Marshall Planner: The Perfect Query Letter on page 111, and Appendix A), and you will definitely need a cover letter (see the Marshall Planner: The Perfect Cover Letter on page 114, and Appendix B), and you may need a synopsis (see page 89, the Marshall Planner: The Perfect Synopsis on page 112, and Appendix C) or a short synopsis (see page 98, and Appendix D); so it's a good idea to have all of these ready before you begin.

Small or Specialized Publishers
The smaller publishers—and today there are more than ever, most of them outside New York City—are usually perfectly happy to accept submissions directly from writers. In fact, I have found that many of them are intimidated by literary agents, and *prefer* to work directly with writers.

You can find the names and addresses of smaller publishers, from regional presses to university presses, in the directories listed on page 131. If you believe that your novel has a niche audience that makes it right for one of these publishers, or will have a regional appeal that makes it a good bet for a local publisher, try submitting directly. Unless you have good reason to do otherwise, begin with a query letter (see chapter twelve) and follow up as appropriate.

Major Publishers Willing to Work Direct

There are still some major publishers that state openly that they are willing to receive material directly from writers. This does not mean they are happy to receive unsolicited manuscripts. It means they are willing to receive query letters from writers, and will ask to see manuscripts that sound promising. When you submit your manuscript in response to an editor's invitation to do so, it becomes *solicited*.

In directories like *Writer's Market*, you can learn whether a publisher is open to unagented submissions. You can also visit the Web site of a publisher you have in mind; often you will find submission guidelines. Submission policies differ greatly; a company's preferences always supersede traditional practice.

One notable example of a publisher that not only is open to unagented material but even encourages it (by holding writing contests and competitions periodically) is Harlequin, the world's largest romance publisher, whose divisions include Harlequin itself as well as Silhouette, Mills & Boon, and Steeple Hill. Within these lines are imprints that publish contemporary romance in all its variations, historical romance, romantic intrigue, and mainstream women's fiction. The company does not accept unsolicited manuscripts, but requires a query letter containing specific components, as well as a brief synopsis of your novel.

> **HELPFUL HINT:** Most publishers of genre fiction (romance, mystery, horror, men's adventure, etc.) are open to queries directly from writers.

Special Circumstances

There are other ways to get editors to consider your work without having an agent, even if the editors work for publishers whose official policy is not to accept unagented material.

You may know someone, or know someone who knows someone, whose books are published by one of the major publishing houses. If so, ask that someone for a referral. If that's not possible, ask for permission to use this person's name and send a query letter (with SASE), mentioning that name right up front. Chances are good the editor will agree to look at your manuscript, if only out of politeness.

If you attend a writers conference or convention and meet an editor who publishes the kind of book you've written, ask him for permission to send your manuscript. If he agrees, mail your manuscript the minute you get home, being sure to mention where you met the editor and that he agreed to read your book. Put this information at the very beginning of your cover letter, so that an assistant screening submissions will be sure to see it and place it on the "Look" pile! (See the Helpful Hint on page 124).

Perhaps you happen to know an editor who publishes what

> **HELPFUL HINT:** When you send material in re-
> sponse to an agent or editor's invitation, mark the
> outside of the envelope *REQUESTED MATERIAL.*
> That way your package won't work itself into the
> dreaded slush pile—the stack of unsolicited manu-
> scripts, which receive little or no attention.

you write. If so, simply ask if you can submit your manuscript. Few people put on the spot in this way have the guts
to say no. You'll get a reading, and if your novel is as good
as I hope it is, your friend, relative, or acquaintance will be
happy he said yes.

Oh, What the Heck!

Don't tell, but despite their "official policies," many major
publishers that claim to be closed to unagented material *do*
open query letters, and *do* ask to see manuscripts. If you're
certain a particular editor at a particular publishing company would be perfect for your novel, what have you got to
lose by sending a query and SASE? The worst that can
happen is that you will receive no response.

On the other hand, a few weeks ago I got a call from a
woman whose first approach to an editor at one of New
York's largest publishers was by means of a query letter, without any special recommendation or connection. She and
this publisher have just signed a healthy, two-book contract.

If you don't think the direct route is right for you, read on.
In chapter fifteen, I tell you how to get an agent who's
perfect—at least for you.

CHAPTER 15

How to Get An Agent: Secrets From Someone Who *Is* One

"Why do I need an agent?" many writers ask irritably. "It may take months to find one—months during which I could be looking for a publisher myself."

Yes, it could take months to find one, and in a few cases—depending on what you write—you can find a publisher yourself (see chapter fourteen). But in most cases an agent is a necessary bridge between you and publication. Why?

Lots of reasons. The best one is that the majority of publishers won't even glance at unagented material. So an agent is instrumental in just getting your manuscript in front of an editor's eyes.

But not just any editor. Agents make it their business to know what kinds of books various editors are looking for, and to learn individual editors' tastes. Agents meet or lunch regularly with editors to get to know them and keep abreast of their changing needs.

Agents have become de facto first readers for editors. Editors will place submissions from agents whose taste they respect at the top of their reading piles. Not surprisingly, then, the greater the agent's credibility, the faster your work gets read.

Today, more than ever, you can benefit from an agent's knowledge when it's time to sign your contract. With the advent of e-publishing and print-on-demand, contracts have become more complicated than ever before, and there are more potential pitfalls for the inexperienced writer.

Take, for example, the unagented writer who sold her first novel, a series romance, to a major New York publisher without an agent. The good news was that this was a publisher willing to read unagented submissions, so the writer got in on her own, without having had to spend months looking for representation. The bad news was that she hadn't done her homework about book contracts. She signed a contract containing a clause that said the publisher was under no obligation to revert rights to her book unless the book was unavailable for purchase *in any form*. A short time after her book was published, the company released it in an electronic edition. A year later, the company then made the book available in a print-on-demand edition. In other words, there will never be a time when this book is unavailable for purchase, which means that this author will never get back her rights.

An agent would have known how to fix that reversion clause so that the author was protected.

HELPFUL HINT: Don't be penny wise and pound foolish. If an editor says he wants to make you an offer, don't think, "I'll handle this one myself and get an agent for the next one." By then you may have gotten yourself into so much trouble in your first contract that no agent will want to touch you!

What else do agents do? By talking with editors and other agents, by attending meetings of publishing-related organizations as well as book conventions such as BookExpo America, they keep themselves up-to-date on the ever-changing trends in reading tastes. They know which publishers are starting new lines and closing down others. They are also the first people editors call when they are looking for writers for book projects that have been conceived in-house.

Two weeks ago I received a call from the head of an audio book publisher. She needed four authors—fast—for a special project. After she described her needs, I considered my client list and came up with four writers I felt would be a perfect fit. The publisher agreed, and at this writing each of these four authors is about to sign a five-figure contract.

Agents exploit your work in other markets and media—and I mean "exploit" in the best sense of the word. Agents typically work with subagents to sell your book in foreign countries, and also with agents in Hollywood to sell television or film rights to your work.

Finally, agents take care of all the "housework" related to a writing career. They track payments (sometimes it seems half my secretary's time is spent chasing advance checks); check royalty statements for accuracy; request various necessary tax forms from the IRS to exempt clients from paying taxes to foreign countries in which their books are published; request reversion of rights to clients' books at the appropriate time . . . the list goes on and on. While your agent is taking care of business, you have more time to do what you do best: Write.

Many agents, like me, are former editors, and many who

aren't have a keen editorial eye. So your agent may become your "secret weapon" to help you revise and polish your work so that it's in its best form before it's submitted to publishers.

Agents fight for you. I've mentioned nagging for checks. Agents also mediate when there's a problem between you and your editor (the old good cop, bad cop routine, which always works). They maneuver to get you as much backing as possible from your publisher's sales, publicity, and promotion departments. When you hate your book's jacket or cover, your agent helps to get it fixed—or redone. If your relationship with your editor has deteriorated to the point where you can't work with him anymore, your agent speaks to the higher-ups to get you assigned to a new editor.

Finally, agents are there for advice as you try to make the best decisions for your writing career.

So How Do You Find One?

There are hundreds of literary agents in the United States. You don't need any special kind of license to be a literary agent, which means that literally anyone can call himself one. Naturally, then, there are great agents and there are not-so-great agents. There are even criminal agents. How do you find a great one who will want *you*?

Forget anything you've heard about a literary agent having to be located in New York City. Some of the most successful agents work out of cities such as Washington, DC; Los Angeles; and Minneapolis. These days it's all what you know and who you know, not where you are. (And I'm not just saying that because I work out of Pine Brook, New Jersey!)

How do you begin the search? First, recognize that this almost-always-necessary process of finding a literary representative is not going to take a few weeks. It could take months or even a year. Know that even after you do your homework, you're probably going to have to send out a number of query letters, synopses, and manuscripts before you hook up with the perfect agent.

Therefore, it makes sense to start some kind of record-keeping system to track your submissions and note which agents you've already tried. The Marshall Planner: Submission Log on page 156 should prove helpful in this regard. I would suggest that you photocopy it and use the copy; you may need to fill several sheets before you hit the jackpot.

The Homework

What should you be looking for in an agent? Obviously, you want someone who handles the kind of novel you've written. You want someone who's excited about your work and believes in it, someone who's excited about nurturing your writing career.

"A career?" you say. "But I've only written one book!" True, but agents want clients who will be with them for the long haul—writers who intend to make a career out of writing . . . or at least those who intend to keep writing, even if the income doesn't provide total financial support. Many clients of my agency have been with us in excess of fifteen years; some have been with me since I worked for a large New York literary agency nearly nineteen years ago. As you might imagine, the agent-author relationship often turns into more than just a business arrangement. An agent sometimes becomes a friend. At the very least, you want someone you feel completely comfortable working with, someone you consider a true ally.

Screening Agents

There's an organization based in New York City, but open to
people anywhere in the country, called the Association of
Authors' Representatives (AAR). In order to belong to this organization, an agent or agency must adhere to a strict Canon
of Ethics on which the organization is based. For example, AAR
members may not charge reading or "handling" fees of any
kind, because the organization believes that fees are subject to
abuse—and in many cases, they're right. AAR members may
deduct reasonable expenses (for couriers and photocopying, for
example) from a client's earnings, but otherwise an agent
should make all of his money by selling books.

Restricting your agent search to members of the AAR makes
your life a lot easier from the start, because the unscrupulous
fee-chargers who prey on the dreams of aspiring writers (and
they always seem to pop up) are immediately weeded out.

Please note: Just because an agent or agency does not belong
to the AAR does not mean that agent or agency is unscrupulous. To join the organization, an agent must have sold a
certain number of books within a certain period of time, thus
newer agents may not be able to join right away. Other agents
simply may not wish to join the organization, for whatever
reason; but they still may be completely legitimate.

For our purposes, however, starting with AAR members
makes the hunt much easier. To get a list of AAR members
and learn more about the organization, visit www.aar-online
.org, the association's Web site. There you'll find not only a
member list but also information such as the Canon of
Ethics, qualifications for membership, and a list of questions
to politely ask an agent once he has offered to represent
you. Note that the AAR's member list provides only names,

addresses, level of membership, and a general notation about the type of material the agent handles: literary, dramatic; adult, children's; etc. Print out this list and attach it to your Marshall Planner: Submission Log.

The Search

How do you find out which of these agents handle the type of book you write?

Directories

Start with the excellent directories that list agents and their specialties and are updated annually:

- *Guide to Literary Agents* and *Writer's Market* (Writer's Digest Books). In these two books you'll find not only agents' subject areas but also specific instructions for approaching them. As mentioned earlier, their special requirements supersede any general advice I give you. Also visit www.WritersMarket.com for additional listings from these two books.
- *Literary Market Place (LMP)*. This expensive volume can be found in almost any library's reference department. In its agent listing it provides subject areas of interest, as well as information about agents' affiliations (organizations, subagents, and so on).

Writers Conferences

Every year, hundreds of local, regional, state, and national writers conferences are held across the country. Some are sponsored by specific writers' organizations (such as those for romance or mystery writers) and will therefore have a genre slant. Others, sometimes sponsored by universities, are for writers in general.

Attending as many writers conferences as is feasible in terms of your time and budget is an excellent way to immediately immerse yourself in the world of writing. More to the point, it's a great way to eyeball agents, who attend in the hope of discovering new talent. Agents will give lectures, participate on panels, and present workshops; often they will grant brief one-on-one interviews with writers (see page 64).

How can you find these conferences? You'll find them listed in magazines such as *Writer's Digest* as well as in writers' newsletters. Also, visit http://writing.shawguides.com for an extensive online directory of writers conferences and workshops. You can search by month, focus, state, and even country to find just the right conference or conferences for you.

HELPFUL HINT: Don't overlook fan conventions. Some agents and editors attend these as frequently as they attend conferences. You probably won't find one-on-one appointments there, but you'll be mingling with these professionals in social situations that will give you ample opportunity to pop The Question: "May I send you my book?"

Writing Contests

An often-overlooked method of reaching agents is to enter writing contests, for which the final-round judges often include agents. Writers organizations often sponsor these contests, and you can find out about them by reading organizations' newsletters and checking their Web sites, as well as by reading writers' magazines such as *Writer's Digest.* To automatically receive announcements of writing contests, join the Writing Contests List, a Yahoo! newsgroup that keeps its nearly 1,000 members updated on a nearly daily basis. To join, go to http://groups.yahoo.com/group/writingcontests/.

Obviously, you want a contest for books in your genre; then you want to see if any of the judges are literary agents. Different contests will require different materials. For instance, a "Hottest First Chapter" contest sponsored by a romance writers organization might require the first chapter and a synopsis of the entire novel, or the chapter alone. Other contests ask for complete manuscripts.

If a contest fits your novel, and there's an agent among the judges, why not give it a shot? It could be a foot in the door, especially since agents often pursue people whose work they have judged—even the nonwinners! Just make sure that if you submit a first chapter or first paragraph or anything short of a complete manuscript, there's a complete manuscript backing it up.

A side benefit of entering contests is that the judges usually provide valuable feedback in the form of a memo or a filled-out judging questionnaire. If you don't win a contest but receive feedback from an agent and feel it's valid, you might try revising your manuscript and then querying that agent about it. If you win or are named a finalist in a contest, you should mention this achievement in *all* your query letters.

A few words of caution. First, don't become a contest addict—someone who spends so much time entering contests that he neglects the most important aspect of trying to get published: querying agents and/or editors. Second, some contests are actually scams to collect entry fees (many prestigious contests have no entry fees, or nominal fees in the range of $25 to cover handling), to get you to buy printed anthologies of the winning entries, or to get you to enter a publishing arrangement. Make sure you know up front exactly what is required to enter, and what the prizes are.

Periodicals

I mentioned *Writer's Digest* above, but there are numerous other periodicals that list or mention literary agents, including *ByLine Magazine* and *Publishers Weekly* (which regularly writes up important deals made by agents in its Hot Deals column).

Books Like Yours

Here's an old trick. When you're reading (and if you've read my two previous Marshall Plan books, you know I'm a strong believer in reading books like the ones you want to write) look for acknowledgments and dedications to agents. Make a note of these agents' names on your AAR listing; for example: *Evan Marshall, The Evan Marshall Agency—mystery, romance, commercial fiction.*

The Web

Grab your Google and start searching. Begin with writers' associations; see if they list agents who will be appearing at their conferences, seminars, or workshops.

Once you discover the name of an agent who handles your kind of writing, use the Web to find out more about him or her. Many literary agencies maintain Web sites providing information about the kind of work they represent, their clients, and submission procedures.

This last idea is a little tricky. If you happen to work in a field that would qualify you as a "qualified book trade professional," you're eligible to receive the popular *Publishers Lunch*, an e-newsletter published on weekdays by Cader Books, a successful book-packaging firm located in Bronxville, New York. As of this writing, 18,000 publishing professionals (and I have to assume that some are aspiring writers planning their escape) receive *Publishers Lunch*. Actually, they receive two newsletters: *Daily Lunch* on weekdays, and *Lunch Weekly* on Mondays. *Lunch Weekly* is chock-full of actual deals agents have recently made, and includes information about the books sold, the editors who bought them, and even the advances paid. If you're eligible, you can subscribe to these free newsletters at www.caderbooks.com.

Armed with information gleaned from the various sources mentioned above, you probably have a list of likely agents for your novel. Now it's time to approach them, and how you do that can make all the difference between landing the agent you want and completely ruining your chances.

You'll find information about planning your submission campaign in chapter thirteen, and about queries and synopses in chapter eleven.

Once you've found an agent who wants to work with you, you'll want to read the following chapter, which tells you how to make sure the relationship goes smoothly and productively.

Section III

THE PROCESS

CHAPTER 16

Making the Marriage Work: How to Partner With Your Agent for a Long, Flourishing Career

In the most effective relationships, each party knows what is expected of him and meets those expectations. Your relationship with your agent will be productive and enjoyable if you understand your respective roles and know standard operating practices.

You've found that path of "yes" after "yes"; an agent is excited about your work and wants to represent you. Now what?

Signing On

Nearly all agents now use a representation agreement. Most offer it at the outset of the relationship, while a few wait until a first sale has been made. Representation agreements range from simple, one-page documents to multipage contracts resembling book contracts. There was a time when agents and writers worked on the basis of an honorable handshake. Now agents—and writers—want everything spelled out in order to avoid disputes or misunderstandings. The representation agreement should state, at the very least, that:

- The agent represents you exclusively; in other words, you can't have two agents at the same time. (In rare cases, a writer may have one agent for fiction and another for nonfiction, or one agent for adult work and another for children's. I don't recommend this kind of setup, which makes it difficult for either of the agents to guide your writing career effectively.)
- The author has final say on all deals negotiated by the agent.
- The agent has the right to work with subagents for the sale of subsidiary rights.
- The agent will receive a commission on deals he or she negotiates, and what that commission will be (usually 15 percent for domestic sales, and 20 percent for foreign—the agent and subagent each receiving 10 percent).
- Either the agent or the writer may terminate the agreement, and what procedures must be followed to do so.
- Disputes between the writer and the agent will be handled in a specific way—for example, by arbitration.

A representation agreement may also state that the agent will keep the writer informed of all business dealings relating to the writer; that the agent will remit all moneys received on behalf of the writer, less commission, within a stated number of business days; and that the agent may deduct, from moneys owed to the writer, charges for reasonable expenses such as photocopying and messenger services.

Below is a copy of the representation agreement I use in my agency.

The Evan Marshall Agency
Author-Agency Agreement

The author signing below (the ''Author'') appoints The Evan Marshall Agency (the ''Agency'') as the Author's exclusive agent to represent the Author and to market throughout the world all writing services by the Author and all rights in and to any and all literary material owned and controlled by the Author, whether alone or jointly with others (subject only to the attached list of exclusions, if any).

The Agency confirms that its individual agents are members of the Association of Authors' Representatives and have signed that Association's Canon of Ethics. The Author shall make all final decisions regarding agreements negotiated by the Agency. The Agency is authorized to handle appropriately all materials received on behalf of the Author and to appoint other parties, including subagents, to assist the Agency in fulfilling this

continued

agreement, but in no event shall the Author be obligated to pay commissions greater than those set forth below.

As compensation for services rendered by the Agency, the Author hereby assigns and transfers to the Agency the right to receive and retain a commission, in the amounts set forth below, on the gross sums payable under all transactions negotiated in the course of Agency's representation of the Author and under any extensions, renewals, revivals, etc., of the same (hereinafter ''Arrangements''). This obligation to pay commissions shall be irrevocable and shall be binding upon the Author's heirs, executors, successors, etc. The Agency's commission on domestic transactions shall be fifteen percent, and on foreign transactions, twenty percent, of such gross sums, prior to deductions from or charges against such moneys. The Author authorizes the Agency to collect and receive in trust on the Author's behalf all moneys due the Author under all such Arrangements and to include in any contract negotiated on the Author's behalf an agency clause incorporating pertinent terms of this agreement. The net due the Author from sums received by the Agency on behalf of the Author will be distributed to the Author within ten business days after actual receipt of funds by the Agency.

This agreement shall continue until the date which is seventy-five days after either party receives written notice of termination from the other. Upon mailing of such notice to Author or upon delivery of such notice to the Agency, the Agency will initiate new business on the Author's behalf only with the express approval of the Author. Notwithstanding any termination of this agreement, the Author shall be obligated to pay the Agency all commissions due the Agency under existing Arrangements. Such Arrangements shall include all deals initiated prior to the delivery of such notice, whether any such deal is formalized prior to or after the termination of this agreement.

All unresolved disputes and controversies in connection with this agreement shall be submitted for arbitration in the City of New York, in accordance with the Commercial Arbitration Rules of the American Arbitration Association. The outcome of such arbitration shall be final and binding on the parties to the proceeding, in accordance with applicable law.

This agreement constitutes the entire agreement

continued

between the Author and the Agency, supersedes for
all purposes all prior understandings, and shall
be governed by the laws of the State of New York pertaining to contracts entered into and performed
within that State.

AGREED:

_____

Dated: _____
Author
Social Security or Tax ID Number:

_____

For The Evan Marshall Agency

_____

Evan Marshall
Its *President* _____
Dated: _____

Communication Is Everything

Once you're officially on board with an agency, it's perfectly
acceptable to have a conversation with the agent to come to
an understanding about your method of working together. For
instance, you might let the agent know that you want to be
kept abreast of all responses to your work, and would appreciate
receiving copies of all letters the agent receives relating to

> **HELPFUL HINT:** Some writers show their represen-
> tation agreement to a lawyer, which may make
> sense, depending on how complicated the agreement
> is. But don't bring a lawyer in to shadow your
> agent. Literary agents know book contracts better
> than most lawyers. In my experience, a lawyer only
> slows things down and annoys the agent and the
> editor.

your submissions. (Some writers ask me *not* to send them any letters, while others ask to see the positive ones only.)

You might tell the agent you will always work your hardest and do your best work, but that if the agent ever has a problem with something you've written or done, he should feel free to tell you so—because you intend to be just as honest.

> **HELPFUL HINT:** This isn't a pop psych book, but
> I'm going to give you some touchy-feely advice any-
> way: Learn the art of the apology. If you make a
> mistake, be the first to say so, then apologize and
> say it will never happen again. That's all anyone can
> ask of you. On the other hand, to take the dysfunc-
> tional approach and ignore a misstep only breeds ani-
> mosity and resentment.

Communication is the most vital component in the writer-agent relationship. If your material has already been submitted to editors (for example, by you or your previous agent), the agent will need to know that, and also will probably want to know what these editors' responses were. If you meet an editor at a writers conference and he shows interest in your work, by all means let the agent know. Don't, however, ever send material of any sort directly to editors; simply pass the information along to your agent and let him do what you hired him to do.

Likewise, if you hear about an editor who's looking for a particular kind of novel, and yours sounds like it fits the bill, don't call the editor; give your agent this information and let him or her act on it. If an editor approaches you at a conference and asks to see material, or even calls you (it happens), be polite, say you're flattered, and promise to let your agent know of the editor's interest immediately.

> **HELPFUL HINT:** Don't lie to your agent. Writers have been know to lie to their agents about their past relationships with editors, their books' sales information, and earlier contract details. Lying to your agent always backfires. Make him your true ally; tell him everything, however negative or embarrassing, and let him work with it. Better that than for him to call you because he's been caught in *your* lie!

Checking In

Speaking of communication, let's tackle an often-sensitive subject. How often should you call (or fax or e-mail) your agent, and how often should your agent call you? There's no right answer, but most agents agree that calling on an as-needed basis works best.

Let's say your agent has your novel out on simultaneous submission. As responses come in, he lets you know about them. He also sends you copies of rejection letters, and perhaps even calls to let you know an editor is interested in you but doesn't feel this particular project is quite right. The agent is communicating with you on an appropriate, as-needed basis.

Is it necessary for the agent to call you, whether or not he's got something to tell you, every Friday like clockwork? I say—and I think most agents agree with me—no. If this is something you expect from your agent, you'd better get it out on the table at the beginning of your relationship so that you can work out a mutually agreeable plan. Don't ever assume your agent will work in a specific way; doing so usually leads to anger and frustration.

Don't get me wrong—your agent should and will call you with updates, questions, suggestions, and other matters. And you have every right to call (or fax or e-mail, if appropriate) *if you have something specific to discuss*. But don't call just to "see how things are going." You'll soon be regarded as an annoyance and a time waster—the last thing any busy professional needs. The bottom line: Your agent will never waste your time, and you should never waste his or hers. Remember, if your agent is successful—and you wouldn't have wanted to work with this agent if he or she weren't—you're one of a large number of clients, all of whom need attention. See Helpful Hint on page 146.

Is Your Agent Your Editor?

How much should you expect from your agent in terms of editorial feedback? Again, there's no correct answer. It's an issue to be brought up during that initial "relationship" conversa-

HELPFUL HINT: There are other ways to keep yourself in your agent's mind besides calling, faxing, and
e-mailing for updates. First—and this may sound obvious, but many writers don't do it—"cc" your
agent on every piece of correspondence you send to
your editor. Your agent needs to see this communication to be "in the loop" anyway. Second, include
your agent (and your editor, of course) on all of
your promotion lists for postcards, kits, press
releases—whatever you send out. Also send him or
her copies of any publicity you get (articles, profiles,
etc.) Third, send cards on the major holidays; add
a "Thank you!" to your signature. Yes, agents get
paid, but much of what we do we don't get paid
for. A "thank you" goes a long way.

tion. Many agents are former editors, and offer detailed
feedback—even editing—to their clients. Other agents who are
former editors offer more general guidance. Some agents
offer none at all, while there are some I've heard of who insist
on approving all material, including manuscripts under
contract, before that material goes to editors. Find out how
your agent works, let him know your preferences, and
come to an agreement.

You're probably thinking, "But shouldn't I ask all these
questions *before* I get to the representation agreement
stage?" The answer is, yes and no. If you've selected this agent
through careful research (which, ideally, includes speaking
to writers this agent represents) you probably know a lot about

how the agent works already, and his or her methods should make sense to you.

You see, agents want to know that you believe they are the best representatives for you. If an agent expresses interest in representing you, and you *then* make it clear you know nothing about her, the agent will think you drew her name out of a hat. Psychologically speaking, that's not a good way to begin.

The ideal method is to learn as much as you can about agents before you approach them. Then, if one of them offers to represent you, you have only the smaller issues to work out.

Expectations

Your agent should be someone you feel comfortable working with, someone you can talk to freely. You should not be intimidated by your agent, or made to feel you are wasting his time when you call, or that he is always too busy for you. You and your agent should be important to each other, and you should treat each other accordingly—with courtesy and respect.

This said, don't expect too much from your agent. Though some agent-writer relationships last many years, and some writers become good friends with their agents, you should not take advantage of the relationship. Your agent is not your therapist; take your insecurities to a licensed psychologist. Your agent is not your banker, so don't ask for advances on your advances, or loans, or a waiver of expenses because you've had a tight year. Your agent is not your travel agent, so don't ask him to make your travel arrangements or get you tickets to a Broadway show. Unless your agent has truly become your friend, don't expect the things you'd expect from a friend, such as rides from and to the airport, use of a guest room, or a shopping companion during your extra day in New York City.

Like you, the agent is a busy professional. Respect him or her, expect the same respect in return, and there's no reason this relationship shouldn't last many enjoyable, productive years.

CHAPTER 17

Divorce: When It Makes Sense to Move On to a New Agent

Even the best marriages may go bad eventually. Sometimes it makes sense to end your relationship with your agent. To stay with an agent when your relationship is less than satisfactory can harm or even end your writing career.

When It's Time to Leave

Agents are, after all, just people. And being people, they are apt to change.

For example, an agent who was once excited about you and your writing may lose enthusiasm after he has submitted your novel to every editor he can think of, without success. I know agents who lose interest after ten submissions, others who remain firm in their belief in their client's work after forty submissions. It sometimes happens that a novel an agent was once excited about doesn't sell. But remember, if the agent also was once excited about your *writing* he should be calling you to say, "Listen, I've tried everyone I can think of, and unfortunately we've had no offers. What else are you working on, and when can I see it?" If, instead, he doesn't call you at all—or, worse, starts not returning *your* phone calls—

you've got a problem. Most likely, the agent has lost his enthusiasm for representing you.

Agents' fortunes change. I have heard stories about agents just starting out in their careers who excitedly take on writers, only to lose interest in their original clients when they take on more lucrative authors. Agents, being people, need to earn a living, and it's understandable that top-earning writers may take priority. But if your agent no longer has time for you at all, she should tactfully tell you so. Unfortunately, not everyone has the ability to be so forthright, and instead of a frank phone call, you may simply get ignored. If this happens, it's time to leave.

Sometimes, as agents grow more successful, or take on more and more clients in the hope of becoming more successful, they lose track of details. You call your agent to ask what happened with that last submission, and the agent doesn't recall what project you're talking about, let alone where it went. If this happens, it's probably time to bow out.

Sometimes, despite their best efforts to research agents, writers make a mistake. They hire an agent who turns out not to be as effective as they thought. The agent is a poor negotiator, or doesn't stand up for his clients' rights, or doesn't submit to appropriate editors. Here, too, it's time to leave.

It's also time to end the relationship if the agent—a person subject to the same slings and arrows as the rest of us—becomes less than effective for personal reasons. No one likes to kick someone when she's down. On the other hand, writing is a business as well as an art, and you must look out for your own best interests. So in cases like this, you must, as kindly as possible, say good-bye.

HELPFUL HINT: All that said, sometimes it's possible to misread the signs. An agent may simply be going through a temporary difficulty such as a divorce, an illness, or a relationship problem. You may find the agent you're trying to leave begging you to reconsider. If so, hear him out; meet with him if possible. Find out whether the problems can be ironed out, and if you think it makes sense, give him another chance.

Making the Break

Leaving your agent is never easy, but if you know it's something you should do, do it sooner rather than later. How?

First, read the clause in your representation agreement pertaining to termination and follow the procedure it sets forth. In most cases, you'll need to send your agent a letter. Send it by Certified Mail—Return Receipt Requested, even if your representation agreement doesn't require that you do so. Then you'll have proof you sent the letter, and when.

In your termination letter, be straightforward, businesslike, and not unnecessarily cruel (publishing is, after all, a very small business, and you don't want it getting around that you're a heartless monster). Tell the agent you've decided to terminate the relationship because you no longer feel it is to the advantage of either of you.

Though you shouldn't have to, remind the agent she should stop submitting your work immediately. If you don't already have complete lists of where all of your projects have been submitted, ask the agent for them. Then ask that the agent either return or discreetly dispose of all of your material that he has on hand. If the agent has copies of your published books, ask for them, keeping in mind that the agent may want to keep one or two copies for the agency's library.

Acknowledge that the agent will, of course, as stipulated in your representation agreement (and it probably will be), remain the agent of record on any deals she has initiated. However, unless your representation agreement prevents your doing so, make it clear that you are taking back control of all *unsold* rights to the books the agent has placed for you. Some agents believe that, unless they are instructed otherwise, it is all right for them to place ancillary rights to books they have sold, even if the author is no longer a client. If you feel the same way, tell the agent she may continue to market unsold rights to your projects. Either way, make clear what you want.

Some writers, when they leave their agents, no longer feel comfortable about the agent receiving moneys on the writers' behalf and forwarding these moneys less commission. These writers therefore arrange a split of moneys at the publisher: 85 percent goes directly to the writer, and 15 percent goes to the agent. If you would like this arrangement, your publisher will most likely need not only your permission to do so but also the permission of your agent. State in your termination letter that you would like moneys split at the publisher, and that you are enclosing a permission letter for the agent to sign and forward to the publisher. This letter should read something like the following.

```
Ms. Jane Doe
Corsair Publishing, Inc.
One Publisher's Row
New York, NY 10022

Dear Ms. Doe:

We hereby request that you split all future moneys
payable to [your name] for the titles list below
as follows:
      85 percent to [your name]
      15 percent to [agency name]

[List of titles]

Thank you.
Sincerely,


_____
[your signature]


_____
[agent's signature]
```

It's not a bad idea to enclose a stamped envelope addressed to Ms. Doe for the agent to use to send her the letter. You want to make sure it reaches her.

Now that I've told you how to write your termination letter, think about whether you want to combine it with a phone call. Believe it or not, some people do. After all, when you've been working with someone for years, a cold, businesslike letter alone may not seem right. Writers who feel this way sometimes make the call first, then send the letter as a formal follow-up. Other writers send the letter first and say in it that they will call. It takes a lot of guts to make this call, before *or* after the letter, but you may feel it's something the agent deserves, even if you're saying good-bye.

The name of the game in publishing, as in life, is to treat people like people and not to burn any bridges. As I've said, it's a small business. But more importantly, anyone with whom you have had a formal business relationship deserves human, professional treatment at the very least.

> **HELPFUL HINT:** Often agents will ask why a writer has left his previous agent. Be discreet! And don't give any more details than necessary. "We had a communication problem" or "I didn't feel he was submitting my material to the appropriate editors" is enough. Why? Because when we hear writers whine on and on about their previous agent or agents, we immediately think the problem was *you*! Be professional and tactful; don't say anything you wouldn't want to get back to your previous agent.

Finding a New Agent

Chances are good that by the time you leave your agent, you'll know a lot more people in publishing than you did when you started. You may have writer friends who are happy with their agents and wouldn't mind putting in a good word for you. Or you may have heard about an agent and filed his name in the back of your mind (or desk drawer) should the day ever come when you'd need it. Well, that day has come. Start making a list of dream agents and networking to find out who the hot names in your genre are these days. After all, you've been out of it for a while, and things probably have changed.

In addition to networking, you can use the same methods you used when you first looked for an agent (see chapter fifteen), except that now you may have more credits to add to your query letter. Which will increase your chances of landing an agent who's just right for you.

Happy hunting.

Marshall Planner: Agent Submission Log

No.	Agent Address Phone	Material Sent	Date Sent	Response	Date of Response	Follow-Up?	To No.

Marshall Planner: Evaluating Your Agent Relationship

Take this quiz to assess the overall effectiveness of your relationship with your agent. On a scale of 1 to 5 (1 representing EXCELLENT and 5 representing POOR), answer the questions below. If a question is not applicable, give it a score of 3.

Working Relationship

- Does your agent communicate with you to your satisfaction? .... _____
- Does your agent display excitement about your writing? .... _____
- Does your agent respond to your phone calls, e-mails, and faxes within a reasonable amount of time? .... _____
- Overall, do you feel as if you and your agent are equals, and that the two of you have a comfortable working relationship (you don't feel intimidated)? .... _____
- Does your agent seem to have enough time for you—on the phone, for example? .... _____
- Does your agent help guide your career, giving you advice for strategies to reach your writing goals? .... _____

Overall Effectiveness

- Does your agent work hard submitting your material? . . . . ____
- Does your agent appear to be submitting to editors who are appropriate for your work? . . . . ____
- Is your agent a strong negotiator? . . . . . . ____
- Does your agent stand up for you with your publishers, fighting to get better treatment for your books? . . . . ____

Housekeeping

- Does your agent handle your money and paperwork (contracts, royalty statements, tax forms, etc.) properly? . . . . ____
- Does your agent keep track of the details of your business affairs—pending projects, submissions, and so on? . . . . ____

SCORE

12-27: You should probably stay put. It sounds as if all is going well. Congratulations.

28-43: It's not necessarily time to leave, but you and your agent need to discuss ways to improve the relationship. Use the higher-scoring questions above to guide your conversation.

44-60: It's time to terminate! Better read chapter seventeen.

PART THREE

PUBLISHING

How to Have a Long and Productive Writing Career

CHAPTER 18

The Offer: How to Tell a Good One From a Bad One

Once you've got an agent, you don't even have to look at your contracts; that's the agent's job, right?

Wrong. Yes, it's the agent's job to get your contracts into the best possible shape, but a smart writer educates himself about contracts. Why? First, because agents, being people, have been known to miss things or make mistakes. Second, because your agent has negotiated the best possible contract doesn't necessarily mean you're going to like it. Often, after I have sent contracts to a client, he calls me with additional points he wants deleted or negotiated. The best reason of all, though, is that a book contract is a legal document between you and your publisher; you are committing to an obligation. You owe it to yourself to know exactly what you're committing to.

Seller Beware

Obviously, I can't take you through every clause of every publisher's contract, but I can tell you the most important points to watch for.

Format

This clause sets forth the physical form in which you are granting the publisher rights to publish your novel. Many publishers today have the capability to publish books in nearly all formats, so this clause will most likely cover all forms: trade hardcover, trade-size paperback, and mass-market paperback. Be aware that if you grant the publisher the right to publish your novel in all of these formats, the publisher *may* but *is not obligated to* publish your novel in all of them. If it is your understanding that your novel will be published in hardcover, it's not enough that trade hardcover be an option; you need to add language *committing* the publisher to this form.

Languages

What language rights are you licensing to the publisher? You may be granting English language rights only, or you may be giving the publisher control of translation rights as well. Be sure the terms in this clause match your understanding of the deal you or your agent has made.

Territories

This clause sets forth the parts of the world in which your publisher may publish your novel, export copies of your novel, or grant other publishers the right to publish your novel. The minimum territory you could grant to a publisher is the United States, its territories and possessions, the Philippines, and Canada (though some big-name authors in recent years have even reserved Canada and sold these rights separately).

You might grant your publisher not just North America but also the United Kingdom and members of the British Commonwealth of Nations such as South Africa, Australia, and New Zealand. In this case your contract will state that you are granting world rights in the English language.

Additionally, you might be granting your publisher the *non-exclusive* right to distribute your novel in what is known as the open market. The open market is made up of the areas other than the territories granted exclusively to your American and British publishers. In the open market, both the American and British publishers are allowed to sell their editions of your novel. For example, you might walk into a bookstore in the Netherlands and find the American and British editions of your novel side by side on the shelf.

Copyright

Except for rare cases, copyright should be in your name. If the publisher insists on copyrighting your novel in its name, walk. To allow this is to give up all control of rights to your book; the publisher will own it.

Subsidiary Rights

These are rights your publisher may grant to other entities. For example, your publisher may decide to publish your novel in hardcover but to license to another publisher the rights to bring out a paperback edition. Other subsidiary rights typically granted to the publisher include book club rights; second serial rights (a magazine or newspaper excerpt published *after* your novel is published); the right to license selections, abridgements, and quotations from your novel in other books; and nondramatic mechanical-reproduction rights.

Other subsidiary rights are up for negotiation—for example, foreign language rights. Very often, agents retain these rights and work to sell them in cooperation with subagents in foreign countries. If you grant these rights to your publisher to handle, pay attention to the "splits"—the way money made from these sales is divided between you and your publisher. A typical split of foreign translation rights is 75 percent to the author and 25 percent to the publisher.

British rights are also subject to negotiation. If you grant these rights to your publisher, a typical split would be 80 percent to you and 20 percent to the publisher.

Electronic rights have been a subject of fierce contention in recent years, with the advent of the World Wide Web and other technologies. These rights refer to handheld electronic, Internet, and print-on-demand (POD) forms of your book. If you grant control of these rights to your publisher—and publishers often insist on having them—you must be very careful. Your contract will contain a reversion clause (language setting forth the circumstances in which you may reclaim the rights to your novel). Usually this clause will say that as long as the book is available for sale, or "in print," the publisher has the right not to revert rights. If a novel is always available to be downloaded onto someone's e-book reader or handheld computer, or available as a POD edition (which means a publisher can keep no inventory of a book and literally print one copy every time someone orders one), then technically your book will never be out of print. Agents avoid this situation by making certain "in print" means in traditional printed book form; or by adding language that in order to be in print, a book must not only be available for sale but selling a minimum number of copies, or earning a minimum amount of money, during a set time period (a year or half-year, for example).

Audio rights have become increasingly important in recent years, and are also subject to negotiation. Many publishers now have audio divisions, and want to control these rights in order to create audiobook versions of the novels they publish. In this case, the usual split is fifty-fifty.

Then there are the subsidiary rights an author or his agent always retains. The most important of these are performance rights (film or television) and commercial/merchandising rights (products based on your novel like toys, action figures, calendars, and so forth—think Harry Potter).

Keep in mind that if you grant control of subsidiary rights to your publisher, and your publisher is successful in selling them, your share is applied to your royalty account if you have not yet earned back your advance.

> **HELPFUL HINT:** If you don't have an agent, you might as well let your publisher control your novel's subsidiary rights. After all, you have no way of handling these rights yourself. Just make sure the "splits" are fair.

Royalties

Except under very special circumstances (for example, when you are to receive a flat fee payment for your novel—a rare occurrence), you will receive royalties, or a specified amount of money for each copy of your book sold.

There are two kinds of royalties: *list* and *net*. Agents and editors like the first kind better. List royalties are calculated on your novel's jacket or retail price. Net royalties are calculated on the amount of money your publisher actually *receives* on each sale of your book, which is a lot less than the jacket price. Most large commercial publishers pay list royalties. Smaller publishers and some publishers of business, professional, and technical books pay net royalties. Neither type of royalty is bad; it's just important that you know which kind you're getting.

List royalties are pretty standard. The typical hardcover list royalty is 10 percent on the first 5,000 copies sold; 12.5 percent on the next 5,000 copies sold; and 15 percent on all copies sold thereafter. If your contract provides for list royalties but doesn't conform to this standard schedule, ask your agent (or your publisher, if you're working without an agent) why.

Typical list royalties for trade paperbacks are 7.5 percent, sometimes "breaking" to a higher rate such as 10 percent at, say, 10,000 or 20,000 copies. Sometimes an additional break to 12.5 percent is seen, or the royalties will start at 10 percent instead of 7.5 percent. It's all open to negotiation.

On mass-market paperbacks, the standard list royalty is 8 percent on the first 150,000 copies sold, and 10 percent on all copies sold thereafter. However, several major New York publishers pay a straight 6-percent royalty, or 6 percent breaking to 8 percent at a negotiable number of copies sold, such as 150,000, 100,000, or even 75,000. One major publisher starts its royalties at 6 percent and keeps stepping them up at 100,000-copy levels until 10 percent is reached.

Again, make sure you know whether your royalty is based on the list price of your novel or the publisher's net receipts.

I won't provide typical net royalties here because in my experience there aren't any typical net royalties. The goal, if you sell to a publisher that pays this way, is to negotiate your percentage as high as possible to compensate for the lower payment structure.

Speaking of royalties, watch out for one of every agent's enemies: joint accounting. You may also hear it referred to as basketing, basket accounting, cross-collateralization, or general accounting. Whatever it's called, it means that if your book does not earn back its advance, the publisher may recoup this unearned money from your other books it has published. Clearly, this arrangement places less risk on the publisher, but it should be avoided.

Each book should have its own life, its own accounting, and have nothing to do with any other book. If you are fortunate enough to land a multibook contract, make sure there is no joint accounting between the books in this contract and other books you have written or may write, and no joint accounting between the books within this contract. Most agents, in order to make it explicit that this practice will not be implemented, request that a sentence be inserted in the contract reading: *This Work* (or *these Works*) *shall be separately accounted.*

In a multibook contract, we also make it clear how an advance is apportioned. For example, if you have received a three-book contract, with an advance of $5,000 per book, it's important that it be stated somewhere in the contract that the advances are apportioned $5,000 for Book 1, $5,000 for Book 2, and $5,000 for Book 3. Why? Because it may not be mentioned anywhere else. Your advance payout (the schedule for disbursing portions of your advance) may bear no resemblance to the actual apportionment. For instance, on this $15,000 contract you might receive $7,000 on signing, $3,000 on delivery and acceptance of Book 1, $3,000 on delivery and acceptance of Book 2, and $2,000 on delivery and acceptance of Book 3.

The Advance

The advance is a down payment against money you'll earn from royalties as well as from your share of subsidiary rights income. Theoretically, the advance represents the amount of money your publisher estimates your novel will safely earn in royalties. Though we regularly hear stories of gigantic advances being paid for first novels (in these cases the publisher has based its advance not on its estimate of earnings but on its *hope* of earnings!), most writers receive modest advances for first novels, often less than $10,000 (sometimes *far* less).

It's to your advantage to negotiate your advance as high as possible, for several reasons. First, because . . . well, it's just nice to have more money! Second, because if your novel does not earn out its advance, you are not obligated to return to the publisher the unearned balance (the portion that has not been earned back). This means you've received some extra money, not necessarily that the publisher has lost money. (If your book *does* earn out its advance, then you have received the money—and made interest on it—that much earlier.) Third, often publishers that have paid a larger-than-usual advance for a novel feel they must try harder than usual to make that novel sell. Most editors will swear up and down that this is untrue, that the measly $1,500 advance they're offering you has no relationship to how hard they'll work to promote your novel. They're lying. Rest assured that a novel that has received a tiny advance will receive a tiny promotion—or, more likely, no promotion at all. Conversely, a novel that has received a whopper of an advance will receive a whopper of a promotional campaign. It's business, pure and simple.

An important element in your quest for the highest possible advance is knowing the going rate for books in your genre. Also factor in whether or not this is your first published novel; a brand-new name is always risky for a publisher. If this is not your first published novel, keep in mind that the sales of your previous book or books will of course have a bearing on what your publisher offers you now. Your agent will know a fair advance to expect for your novel. If you're working without an agent, this is a good time to do some research and networking.

> **HELPFUL HINT:** A huge advance is not always a good thing. Consider the author who held out for a large advance on her novel, which then sold abysmally. The publisher—as publishers are wont to do—blamed the author and never wanted to hear her name again. Sometimes it makes sense to settle on a reasonable advance and collect any royalties beyond that later.

The Payout

Okay, you've come to terms on your advance, but how and when will you get it? This, as I mentioned above, is called the payout. There's no one right payout. For a single, completed first novel, an excellent payout would be half of your advance when you sign your contract, and the other half when you deliver a revised manuscript that is acceptable to the publisher (yes, undoubtedly there will be revisions to do).

But publishers, like everyone else, like to hold onto their money as long as possible, which means stretching out pay-outs as long as they can. So, a possible payout for the same novel might be a third of the advance on signing, a third on delivery and acceptance of a revised manuscript, and a third several months (the number to be negotiated) after this acceptance. What agents try to avoid is payment on publication, since publishers' contracts allow them two years or more in which to publish a book. That's a long time to wait for your money. On the other hand, major six-figure deals often include payouts that include payment on publication—far more palatable when each payment is large.

The Option

Some contracts call this the Right of First Refusal. Whatever it's called, it gives your publisher the right to be the first to consider and make an offer on your next project. The thinking behind the option is that a publisher that has invested time and money in an author wants the opportunity to keep publishing that author, either to have more time to receive the fruits of its efforts, or (if your first book has done well) to get even more, uh, fruit.

Be careful with this one! Mess it up and you could be in trouble for a long time.

There are several factors to keep in mind as you negotiate your option.

Is the option on your next work, or on more than one? It should be on only your next book.

But what kind of book? A fair option, in my opinion, is on the author's next book of the type that's being sold in the current contract. In other words, if the novel you're selling to a publisher is a "sweet" contemporary romance of 55,000 words, then the option should be on your *next* "sweet" contemporary romance of 55,000 words—not on your next romance. Publishers will try to get an option on the next book in the same genre, the next novel, or even the next book-length work. Limit the option so that it's on the same type and length of work being sold. Then you'll be free to sell other kinds of books, or the same kind of book but in a different word length, to other publishers.

When does the option commence? This is a tricky one. Often, publishers will try to get you to accept an option that doesn't start until the book you're selling now has been published. As I've mentioned, publishers these days have two years or more to publish a book, so if you agree to this option, you've doomed yourself to waiting until your book is out before you can sell another book. Other publishers may try to get you to agree to an option that starts a month or several months after the book you're selling now has been accepted. No good. The option should start *immediately* after acceptance of the work you're selling now—period.

What kind of material, exactly, must you show the publisher to satisfy your option? Publishers often try to word the option so that you must submit the complete manuscript of your next work. You should not have to do this. Once your first novel is published, you should be able to make sales on the basis of a proposal: a synopsis and sample chapters, or even just a synopsis. If you despise synopses and enjoy completing manuscripts, that's your prerogative, but you shouldn't be obligated to finish your novel to secure a contract.

Is the option on books written under just the name or pseudonym you're using in this contract, or for anything you write under any name? Some publishers care only about getting a crack at the next book under the same name as the one going on the current work; others want a chance at everything. Just make sure you know what *you* want (for example, you might want to write books in another genre, under another name, for another publisher), and be sure you understand and can live with the terms to which you're agreeing.

Ideally, the option should be a "first-look option" only. This means that after a specified amount of time, (assuming the publisher wants the book under option) if you and your publisher are unable to come to terms, you can walk away without any further obligation to the publisher.

But publishers have been known to slip in wording that turns these options into veritable tar babies. The first of these mutations is the "matching option." It stipulates that if you and the publisher are unable to come to terms, you may submit your material elsewhere, but if you receive an offer, your original publisher has the right to buy the book for the same terms offered by the other publisher.

I'm sure you can see the disadvantages to this form of option. Ethically, you must inform new publishers that if they make an offer, your original publisher has the right to take the material away from them for the same amount. Few publishers want to bother investing time to consider a proposal that is likely to be snatched away.

Another variation is the "10 percent topping option," which

works like the matching option, except that the original publisher can take the book for an advance that is 10 percent higher than the advance offered by the new publisher. For the same reasons, this is also bad news.

Particularly evil is an option that states that the publisher has the right to the author's next work *on the same terms and conditions* as those for the present work. You want this out. As your career progresses, you deserve the improved terms success brings.

What should the option say? A good option clause might read something like this:

> The Author grants [publisher] the exclusive option to acquire the same rights as have been granted in this Agreement to the Author's next work of [genre] of [word length] written under the name [name or pseudonym used for the current work]. [Publisher] shall be entitled to a period of forty-five (45) days after submission of a synopsis and sample chapters for this next work in which to make an offer for that work, during which time the Author agrees not to solicit any third party offers, directly or indirectly. If [Publisher] wishes to acquire the next work, the Author and [Publisher] will attempt to reach an agreement as to terms during a thirty (30) day period of exclusive negotiation. If they cannot reach an agreement, the Author shall be free to submit the next work elsewhere, but the Author may not accept an offer from any

other publisher on terms equal to or less
favorable than those offered by [Publisher].
[Publisher] shall not be required to consider
the Author's next work until its acceptance of
the complete manuscript of the present
Work.

Note that the author may not accept an equal or lesser offer
from another publisher—not an unreasonable demand. This is
not the same as having to take a new offer back to the original
publisher to be matched or topped by 10 percent.

> **HELPFUL HINT:** It's tricky to write for two publishers at the same time unless you are exceptionally prolific. Even then it's usually advisable to write under two different names. Why? Because if one publisher doesn't promote you as hard or as effectively as the other, that publisher's bad sales figures will hurt your sales at your *other* publisher. In addition, publication dates often conflict; you don't want two of your own books coming out *too* close together, or you're competing with yourself. If you do write for two houses, details of scheduling can be handled by your agent.

Termination

I suppose this is like thinking about someone's death before
he is even born, but the fact is, most books do eventually
go out of print. If and when your novel goes out of print, you

should be able to get back your rights, perhaps to sell to another publisher. This issue is covered in your contract's termination clause.

Some publishers use a termination clause that simply states that if your book is not in print (meaning commercially available for sale) after a specified amount of time from publication (for example, three or seven years), then rights automatically revert to the author.

Most publishers, however, don't make it so easy. The reason is that even if your novel is out of print, it's advantageous for a publisher to still have it under contract, against the possibility that you will hit it big, or that changing tastes will bring novels like yours back into demand.

It all boils down to the definition of "out of print." Publishers usually try to say a book is in print if it is on sale by the publisher *or* if any contract for its publication is outstanding—in other words, if a contract for licensed rights is still in effect. You should try to remove the second part, though some publishers will fight you on it.

Ideally, of course, you or your agent should be able to request reversion of rights to your novel as soon as it is no longer available for sale; however, most publishers will make you wait a specified amount of time before you can ask. If so, try to make this amount of time as short as possible, perhaps three years.

The termination clause should say that within a specified period of time (for example, sixty days from your written request) the publisher must inform you that it will reprint your book (also within a specified period of time) or else revert your rights.

With the advent of electronic rights and print-on-demand publishing, it has become frighteningly easy for publishers to keep books "in print." As discussed on page 162, you should get around this by stipulating that to be considered in print, your book must not simply be available for sale but also be selling a certain number of copies or earning a certain amount of money within a specified period (for example, a statement period, which is six months; or a year).

HELPFUL HINT: If your book is out of print, get the rights back as soon as you can. Better the book should be on your or your agent's shelf, ready to be purchased by a new publisher, than languishing out-of-stock at the original publisher. Additionally, a request for reversion of rights often gooses a publisher into reprinting—a good thing.

Negotiating Your Own Contract

If you approach a publisher without an agent and are offered a contract, be careful. At this point some authors call a few of the agents on their wish list and explain that they have an offer but need representation. Sometimes the agent will bite, sometimes not. If you intend to contact an agent once you receive an offer, do not accept any of the publisher's terms until you've done so. Once a term has been accepted, an agent you bring in later cannot ethically change it. Simply say something to the effect of, "I'm delighted you would like to publish my book. I intend to bring in an agent and will get back to you shortly." No honest publisher should have a problem with this.

If you get an offer but can't interest an agent or would rather work without one, do your homework, including a careful review of the guidelines above. Know what to expect as a reasonable advance for a first novel in your genre, as well as what competitive royalties are. If you do not have an agent to handle your novel's subsidiary rights, there's nothing wrong with granting control of these rights to the publisher; just make sure you know what fair splits of the proceeds should be.

In general, take your time in negotiating the deal. Don't get so caught up in the excitement of receiving an offer, or so overcome with gratitude, that you rashly accept something you don't understand.

First will come the "deal points," or the main points of the contract. Write them down and say that you will get back to the editor as soon as possible; then check your notes and do your research. If you feel some things need alteration, call the editor and politely list the changes you are requesting. You may get a yes, you may get a no, or you may have to negotiate. As I've said, take it slowly.

Later, after the deal points have been negotiated, you'll receive several copies of a book contract in the mail from either your editor or the publisher's contracts department. Once again, consult your notes and research materials, then get back to the person who sent you the contracts and work out any changes you want to the best of your ability.

> **HELPFUL HINT:** If your novel has been published by an established American publisher, consider joining The Authors Guild (www.authorsguild.org). It sends new members an informative packet of information including a sample contract, and even offers advice on individual contracts.

CHAPTER 19

Making the Most of Your Editor

Your agent isn't your only ally in the publishing process. So is your editor. In fact, even if your agent is the staunchest of supporters, you're in trouble if your editor isn't fully behind you. In this chapter I'll tell you how to make sure your editor is on your team to ensure the most successful possible publication for your novel.

First, consider the editor's job. It is to acquire books that sell well and make money for his company. Books that sell well are well-written books. The easier authors are to work with, the more books an editor is able to acquire. So logic tells us that an editor who helps his authors produce the best-written books possible, and whose authors are so easy to work with that the publication process always goes smoothly and their books are published frequently, is a successful editor. Editors, like all career professionals, want to be successful. They want to rise through the ranks and attain a reasonable salary in this notoriously low-paying field. Just think of Vidal Sassoon's marketing campaign slogan from the late 1980s: "If you don't look good, we don't look good." It applies just as aptly to editors.

How do you become one of these desirable authors? Let's take it a step at a time.

Understanding the Process

Your novel has been accepted by an editor. *Your* editor. If you have won a contract on the basis of a complete manuscript, the editor will undoubtedly have some revisions in mind; no manuscript is absolutely perfect the first time around. If you have sold on the basis of a proposal, you'll complete the book and *then* have to do revisions.

How will you receive these revision instructions? Your editor will most likely have a general conversation with you in which he goes over the main points of his revision suggestions. Soon after that, you should receive a revision letter; refer to it carefully as you make your changes.

A revision letter, if an editor is smart, usually begins with praise for the novel; and why not? After all, the editor has bought it because he loves it. Next come general comments. For example, the editor might suggest that a certain character be played down, or warmed up; or that the pacing in your novel's beginning be picked up a bit. These changes will require that you read your novel through and make changes you feel will achieve the effects the editor is looking for.

After the general comments invariably come the line-by-line points. These are questions, comments, requests for fact- or logic-checking, suggestions of any sort—but in specific places in your manuscript. For instance: *Page 236, second paragraph: Wouldn't Agnes mention having seen Bernie at the hotel that morning?* Or: *Why does Eddie react so angrily here? Doesn't seem believable.*

Finally, your editor will write comments or suggest changes

right on the manuscript itself, either by writing in the margin or between the lines (see why you need wide margins and double spacing?) or by affixing query slips or Post-It Notes to the pages.

> **HELPFUL HINT:** As soon as you receive your revision letter, call, e-mail, fax, or write to your editor, expressing your thanks for the careful reading and hard work he's obviously put in. When you send back your revised manuscript, thank him again and let him know that you believe (as I hope you will) that his suggestions have made your novel better.

Often, when I have sold a first novel for one of my clients, the writer will ask me if he has to make all of the revisions his editor has suggested. No, of course not; it *is* the writer's book, and the writer must agree that the revisions are called for. If you disagree with something your editor suggests, or you believe the editor has requested a particular change because he's missed something in your manuscript, you have every right to courteously point this out.

Remember, though, that people get to be editors—most of the time—because they have a talent for making books better. In other words, keep an open mind; get some distance from your book if you can; try to be objective and decide whether the editor has raised some valid points. It's human nature not to want to dig back into a manuscript once you're finished with it. You must put aside this natural resistance to doing more work on your novel (rather than starting the new one you're itching to get on paper) and accept that the process isn't over. You must also accept that you will probably go through the revision process with every novel you write.

Your editor will undoubtedly ask you to deliver your revised manuscript by a certain date; frequently this date will already be stated in your contract. Work hard to meet this deadline, as you should work hard to meet *all* deadlines (more on this subject below). Your editor will expect a complete, revised manuscript, not the original manuscript with inserts (unless the revisions requested are truly minimal). Send him this revised manuscript, along with a cover letter expressing your thanks for his input and (if applicable) explaining why you didn't do anything you didn't do.

But I thought editors didn't edit anymore. We hear this a lot lately. Is it true? In a way, yes. But in my experience, it actually means not that editors do less work on the books they acquire, but that they are more apt to acquire the books that need the least amount of work. An especially candid editor once said to me, "I need manuscripts that are basically ready to go, nice and clean. A quick line edit, a light copyedit, and off it goes to the typesetter."

Yikes, that sounds like a lot to ask. Yes, it is, but it's the reality of publishing today. That's why you must deliver the most polished manuscript you can; never turn in a piece of work you know still needs work, expecting your editor to do it. Do that a few times and you may find yourself looking for a new publisher.

Now what happens? If you've done the careful, conscientious job I know you'll do, the editor will be satisfied with your revisions. Now it's time for him to line-edit your manuscript. The amount of line editing your manuscript receives will vary according to the quality of your writing and the tendencies of your editor.

In the old days, the editor showed the author the line-edited manuscript before sending it to the copyeditor. In these streamlined times, however, the manuscript will usually go directly from the editor to the copyeditor. The copyeditor is the person who makes your manuscript as close to perfect as possible, correcting mistakes in spelling and grammar, correcting inconsistencies, "styling" the manuscript (marking elements such as chapter heads for the book designer), and asking you questions in the form of queries—questions written directly on the manuscript pages or, more often, affixed to them by means of query slips or Post-It Notes.

At almost all publishing companies, it's house policy to send the copyedited manuscript to the author. However, some publishers (usually companies that publish primarily paperback-original genre fiction) do *not* send the author the copyedited manuscript unless he specifically requests it. Make a point, then, of asking when you turn in your revisions whether you will see the manuscript at this stage.

How can those few publishers who skip this stage address the copyeditor's queries if they don't send the manuscript to the author? The editors deal with the queries themselves. As much as I trust my editors, this would make me nervous. I always ask to see my copyedited manuscripts, and you should, too.

What happens if you don't see your copyedited manuscript? You won't see the book again until it has gone through the next stage—typesetting. After this stage, your editor sends you page proofs, which are your novel's actual pages as they will look in the final, printed book, but usually on 8.5″ × 11″ paper. (The days of galleys—long sheets of print, not yet broken into pages—are over.) The trouble with not seeing your manuscript before it's typeset is that if you find something you don't like in your page proofs, it may be too late to fix it. Publishers allow very little in the way of changes to page proofs; some publishers allow only the correction of typographical errors. You don't want to be presented with a bad surprise you can't do anything about.

You've seen your copyedited manuscript, then, and now you're looking at page proofs—which is pretty exciting, because now your words are set in type; they look like a book!

At this stage, as with the copyedited-manuscript stage, your editor will give you a deadline. Meet it or beat it. Publishers' policies about page proofs vary. Some ask authors to return the entire set of page proofs; others want only the pages bearing changes mailed or faxed to them. Your page proofs will come with a letter, usually from someone in your publisher's production department, outlining the house's policy. Follow it.

You've carefully corrected your page proofs and returned them. Now comes a seemingly endless wait. You may wonder why on earth the publisher needs so much time between the day you turned in your page proofs and the publication date your editor has given you. Here's why:

What Happens Now?

Lots of important work is done during this time; you just may not see it. For example, your editor will attend a meeting to discuss ideas for your novel's jacket (if it's a hardcover) or cover (if it's a paperback). Before this meeting, your editor may ask you for input.

Be careful here. The editor is not asking you to tell him exactly how you want your jacket or cover to look, or to send in a sketch or painting. He just wants *ideas*. In the end, your publisher will decide how your book will look.

Many new authors get nervous at this stage. *What if they put an awful jacket on my book?* they ask. It's unlikely your jacket will be awful, but it's highly likely it will be something you're not expecting. At this stage it's important to remember that publishers are in the business of packaging novels for optimum sales. Let them do their job. Chances are your editor will send you preliminary sketches, or your cover art, or perhaps an early jacket proof. He's not sending it for your approval, but for your information. Only the very top authors get jacket or cover approval guaranteed in their contracts; others who insist on being involved in the process get "jacket (or cover) consultation," which in effect is meaningless. A publisher may "consult" with you and then do whatever he wants.

On the other hand (and there always seems to be one, doesn't there?), you may truly hate your jacket or cover, and for legitimate reasons. It happens. If so, call your agent, not your editor, and have a conversation about the problem. Decide with your agent on the best strategy for approaching the editor with your complaint. Usually it's the agent who calls the editor and works to get changes made; this is one of the things agents do best.

But coming up with a jacket or cover isn't all that happens while you're waiting for your novel to be published. Copy must be written for the jacket flaps (for a hardcover) or back cover (for a paperback). Here, again, your editor may run this copy past you—but he is not asking for your approval. He wants to know if there are any glaring inaccuracies. There may be, because very often this copy is written from your synopsis, and any writer knows that books often end up deviating from their synopses.

Did you change a name when you wrote the book? Decide on a different setting? Remove an incident that's now front and center in the cover copy? If so, your editor needs to know about it. What he doesn't need to know is that you think the copy takes a completely wrong tack, or that it gives away too much of the story, or leaves out its most wonderful feature. As I said above, leave this function to your publisher, who knows what works best in terms of selling books.

HELPFUL HINT: You will, of course, avoid scenarios like the one described above if you stick as closely as possible to your synopsis as you write your novel. If, as you're writing, a major deviation occurs to you, run it past your editor to make sure he thinks it's a good idea.

Your editor may very likely run the catalog copy for your novel past you. This is the text that appears in the publisher's catalog, which is distributed to booksellers. In showing you this copy, your editor is not asking you if you like the approach—that's already been decided on in-house. He's asking if you spot any egregious errors or omissions. Help your editor by responding swiftly and constructively. Once again, give your publisher credit for knowing the best angle to take to sell as many copies of your novel as possible.

Still more things happen during your novel's lead-in time. The book is presented to the company's sales representatives at the semiannual sales conference, usually by your editor. Other departments make plans to do their jobs with respect to your book. For example, if it is decided that advance reading copies

(ARCs, as we call them) of your book will be sent to periodicals that review books (such as *Publishers Weekly*, *Kirkus Reviews*, and *Library Journal*) as well as to newspapers and booksellers, the publicity department will create these. Usually these will be sent out with a press release and additional items such as an author bio sheet and perhaps your photograph.

The promotion department may decide to create bookmarks or postcards for your novel, and these things also take time.

But don't get the wrong idea. If this is your first published novel, the harsh reality is that it will probably receive little in terms of publicity and promotion beyond the basics I've discussed above. Today, publishers' budgets are skewed toward the names at the top of the list: the big brand-name bestsellers. Little money is left for the books underneath.

That's why you'll need to embrace the concept of self-promotion—appearing at conferences and conventions, holding book signings at local bookstores, speaking at libraries or to civic groups. . . . The only limits to what you can do are your time, energy, and money.

But be careful. Be sure to let your editor know that you plan to do some self-promotion, and ask him about the correct protocol for this situation. Should you send a memo to the publicity and promotion directors outlining your plans? If you live close enough, should you try to set up a meeting with your publisher? Should everything go through your editor?

Keeping Your Editor on Your Side

When I was an editor, it was strict policy at one of the companies I worked for that an author should *never* contact anyone except his or her editor. The editor was *never* to refer an author to other departments. In other words, the editor

HELPFUL HINT: Don't get in touch with your editor and/or your publisher's publicity and promotion departments until you have *all* of your plans for self-promotion set. Nobody wants information in dribs and drabs.

was the only conduit between the author and the rest of the company. Other companies are not quite so strict about this, but it's still basically how they all work. Your editor is your champion, your advocate; he's in charge of you, so to speak.

That's why you need to make sure he's your friend.

How can you do that, aside from the ways I've outlined above? Here are some specific tips, some of which may relate to what I've already told you:

Be Proactive

Don't be pushy, telling your editor how to do his job, but don't be completely passive, either. For example, sooner or later your editor will need a brief biography to run in or on your book. Left to his own devices, he might compose one from whatever he finds in your file—your query letter or cover letter, or your agent's cover letter. Take control of the situation by studying bios in other novels and composing your own bio. There are probably things about your life your editor doesn't know but which would improve the bio. Editors don't always think to include your e-mail address, or your Web site's URL. If you would like to plug your site and receive e-mail from fans, include this information.

I mentioned above that your editor may ask you for input on your jacket or cover. If, after your manuscript has been accepted, no such request has been made, and you have what you think is a great idea for a jacket or cover treatment, there's nothing wrong with sending your editor an e-mail or letter outlining your ideas. You might even include jackets and/or covers of books that have the look you're after. But then pull back and let your editor and the art department do their thing.

Keeping in mind that if you're new to the game, your novel probably won't get much of a budget for publicity and promotion, don't hesitate to let your editor know of any low- or no-cost ideas you have for pushing your book. For example, one of my clients, a writer of culinary mysteries that contain recipes, suggested to her publisher that they create "recipe cards" to promote her novels in bookstores. The publisher loved this idea and has implemented it for each of her last three novels, at minimal cost.

Being proactive means that if you're visiting your publisher's city, you should let your editor know ahead of time and, if possible, set up a meeting—breakfast, lunch, drinks, coffee, dinner, or just a friendly drop-in at the office if he's really pressed for time.

Whatever meeting you schedule, it's always a good idea to arrange to meet your editor at the office ahead of time; then you can get the "grand tour" and meet your editor's colleagues if you've never visited your publisher's offices, or renew acquaintances if you have. When you visit, a small gift for your editor is never a bad idea; it shows you appreciate him and the time he's taking for you.

Being proactive also means supplying your publisher with

HELPFUL HINT: Don't forget the gatekeeper: your editor's assistant! Getting on this person's good side can be instrumental to a successful relationship with your editor. If you send your editor a holiday card, send one to his assistant, too. If you take a gift to your editor, take his assistant something—though not necessarily as lavish. Most people forget assistants, so your gesture will be greatly appreciated.

---

the names and addresses of people the publisher wouldn't think of who should receive a copy of your book. Usually, when you sign your contract, you will receive an author questionnaire that requests this kind of information. Don't assume that at the appropriate time that questionnaire will be whipped out of your file and consulted. Sometimes, depending upon the efficiency of a publicist or promotion staffer, an author questionnaire never leaves its file. For this reason, don't be embarrassed about sending lists of names you've already included in the questionnaire. Just in case the questionnaire *has* been consulted, state in your cover letter that you have already provided these names and are resending them as a convenience.

Proactive also means being assertive. All of the above advice notwithstanding, if you learn of something regarding your novel with which you violently disagree, you owe it to yourself to make your feelings known—tactfully.

Remember, it's at times like these that your agent earns his commissions, so make full use of him. He knows how best to present your wishes so that there is the greatest possible chance of their being respected.

If you believe a matter would be better handled directly between you and your editor, speak to him in an honest, nonpersonal way. Tell him what he's done that you object to and how it makes you feel; ask him to please not do it again. Easier said than done, I agree; but it's a skill worth learning. Dysfunctional relationships between writers and editors only get worse and worse, and ultimately fall apart completely.

Give Your All

It should go without saying that you should give your all, do your very best work. Sadly, however, in my years as an editor, packager, and agent, I've seen so many cases in which writers have *not* done their best work that I explicitly give you this advice now.

How can you give your best work? To begin with, give yourself enough time; use the full amount of time given to you in your contract. If you have been given two months for revisions, start right away and use those two months. If you have sold your novel on a proposal and have been given ten months to complete the manuscript, use those ten months. Don't do what too many writers do and procrastinate, so that revisions are completed in a week-long whirlwind and manuscripts are completed in three sleepless weeks. It's impossible to deliver your best writing under these circumstances. The rushing itself compromises the quality of your work, not to mention that you'll have no time to let your material rest before you begin to revise it slowly and thoughtfully.

Giving your all also means undertaking the revisions suggested by your editor with an open mind and a willingness to work hard. Your editor has not suggested these revisions simply to enslave or punish you. He truly believes they will improve your novel, and chances are good that he's right. Over my years as an agent, occasionally writers have gleefully informed me that their editors wanted few revisions. In many cases, this was because the editor had truly found very little that needed improving. In other cases, however, I knew the truth: that the editor wasn't as thorough as he should have been and simply hadn't taken the time needed to write a thorough revision letter. These editors weren't doing the authors any favors. Revisions are a good thing—a vital part of your editor's job—and you should embrace them and undertake them with gusto. And, of course, you should deliver them on time.

Be Upbeat

By this I mean be someone who's pleasant to work with. Be gracious when your editor or other people at your publishing house ask you for material or information. Don't call anyone unless you've got a good reason; and before you call, consider whether an e-mail, fax, or letter might do the job just as well. Just as an agent has many clients, an editor has many authors, and time is at a premium. If you have a complaint, think about whether it would sound better coming from your agent. Better yet, think about whether you should make the complaint at all.

I've noticed that the more years people spend in publishing, the less tolerance they have for people who are unpleasant. I've heard it called the "life is too short" factor. Of course, a best-selling author who's a pain in the rear end is cut some slack—a bore who's making a lot of money for your company is easier to tolerate than someone who isn't—but eventually, no matter how big you are, it all catches up with you. Ironically, I have found that the most successful authors are also the most gracious and professional ones.

Communicate

Effective communication involves good news as well as bad. If your editor does something for you, thank him. As far as I'm concerned, every novelist should include his editor's name in his acknowledgments; yet often this name is conspicuously absent. Why? Is it because the author feels the editor is paid for his work and doesn't deserve a thank-you? Nonsense. No good editor is adequately compensated for his work, nor does any good editor work only for money.

Bad news must be communicated as well as good—and as quickly as possible, so it's not given a chance to fester and build resentment. Again, make use of your agent whenever possible to communicate negative news.

Healthy communication includes acknowledging when you have made a mistake—and apologizing. We're all human; we all make mistakes. If you've made one, admit it, say you're sorry, ask your editor to please excuse you, and assure him it will never happen again. Then don't let it happen again!

Communication is also just smart business. Stand out from your editor's crowd of authors by periodically reminding him you're out there. If you see a clipping relating to your novel or to the subject of your novel that you think he might find interesting, send it to him with a cheery note. If the editor suffers a personal loss, send a sympathy note. Remember him at the holidays, at the very least with a card. These gestures not only signify that you care about and respect this colleague as a person, but they also keep your name in front of him.

This should go without saying, but include your editor, as well as your publicist and anyone else with whom you've come in contact at your publishing house, in your promotional mailings. Send your editor and publicist reviews you find of your novel; don't assume they've seen them already, or that they know about everything you're doing. Blow your own horn.

Be Reliable

We've talked about meeting deadlines. I can't stress the importance of this enough. Though you may hear nothing from your publisher for months, rest assured the wheels are turning and your book is being worked into a grand scheme that's difficult to change at the last minute. If you know you will be late—say, for example, a relative becomes ill and you know the next several months will be taken up with caring for him—let your editor know immediately so that you can arrange for an extension on your delivery date. If you tell your editor early that you need more time, he can still move books around if necessary, or simply adjust your production schedule. To tell your editor a week before your delivery date that you need another month can be disastrous.

One of my clients, who has delivered every one of her twenty-seven novels on or before their delivery dates, once revealed to me the secret of her reliability: She always asks for far more time than she really needs. Simple but incredibly effective.

Recently, when an editor called me and said she needed a writer for a special project whose schedule would not allow for lateness, I immediately suggested this writer, who got the job. Around the same time, another editor called with a similar project, and I recommended a client I knew would be perfect. To my horror, the editor responded that she had heard that this author was always late. I swore up and down that my client would deliver this project on time (see— agents will even lie for you!), but to no avail. The editor told me in no uncertain terms that she couldn't take any chances. This writer had blown her credibility, not simply with her own publisher but with another she had never written for! Publishing is a woefully small business.

Your publisher will ask you to do many things, and most of the time you will be given formal or informal deadlines. Your line-edited and copyedited manuscript must be reviewed and returned by a certain date. Your page proofs must be turned around in one, two, or three weeks. Your publicist needs that list of clown colleges that should receive press kits about your novel set in the circus world—ideally within the next couple of days. If possible, put down whatever you're doing and help these people by giving them what they need as quickly as they need it. In reality, you'll be helping yourself.

Be Realistic

Get real. If you've done your homework, you know a writer's first few novels aren't likely to get much in the way of publicity and promotion. So don't waltz into your publisher's offices asking where you'll be sent on your ten-city tour. Instead, ask in a nonthreatening, professional way exactly what you can expect. In my experience, everyone knows this information from the start and is glad to share it, even if it's bad news. You should have it, anyway, so you can plan your own self-promotion campaign.

Being realistic also means understanding that different editors have different amounts of autonomy, depending on where they are on the ladder. You may be working with an editorial assistant (yes, once in a while they are allowed to acquire books), an assistant editor, an associate editor, an editor, a senior editor, an executive editor, the editor in chief, the editorial director, the publisher, or some hybrid of two or more of these titles. Depending upon your editor's title, he may or may not have the power to grant your wishes. He may have very little power at all.

Editors low on the totem pole must frequently explain that they must present requests for special treatment to their superiors for consideration; writers often become frustrated at hearing this again and again. Be understanding. Remind yourself that he doesn't like this state of affairs any more than you do. Remember also that in publishing, people rise relatively quickly. Before you know it, that young woman who acquired your first novel as an assistant editor may very well be a senior editor, with more power to give you what you want—and to put that push behind your book. He'll appreciate that you were patient during the ride up.

Understand that editors are notoriously overworked, and that although your editor will try to make you feel as if you're his only author, he will sometimes fail. He may take longer than you would like to respond to a proposal or manuscript, or to answer your phone calls or e-mail. If this happens, give him a gentle nudge; chances are good he'll move you higher on the work pile. In publishing, the courteously squeaky wheel definitely gets the most grease.

It's all common sense, really. Work hard to maintain a good relationship with your editor—your staunch advocate and supporter, your true ally in the adventure of publishing a novel. You'll ensure the most effective publication for the books you work so hard to write. More importantly, you'll reap the most enjoyment from this very special creative relationship.

CHAPTER 20

No Excuses: A Publisher and Format for *Every* Novel

You've queried every agent on your list, and not a single one has taken the bait. Why? Perhaps your query letter isn't quite up to snuff, or your novel doesn't sound as if it will have broad enough appeal, or it doesn't sound fresh enough, or . . .

You've also tried every publisher you could find that's willing to work with authors directly—also without success. And none of your friends or relatives is an agent or an editor, or knows one.

Now what? Are you still passionate about your book? Is it your best work?

Yes? Then there are still avenues to explore.

Self-Publishing

Have you considered traditional self-publishing? The stigma long attached to it has disappeared. It's a lot of work, but it can be fun and extremely gratifying. When you take this route, you are in effect performing the functions of every department at a publishing house in addition to having written the novel.

I recommend hiring a freelance editor and copyeditor to

polish your prose. Then, for the novel's interior as well as its cover, you can hire a designer or take advantage of a designer who works for a short-run (small printing) printing company. Consider the various possible formats (paperback versus hardcover; different trim sizes) and get a handful of bids before committing to a deal. Ask to see examples of books printed by the companies you're considering.

Eventually you'll find yourself with a garage or guest room full of books, and you'll need to find ways to sell them. Set up a Web site. Send postcards to family and friends. Approach local bookstores about taking copies on consignment. Even Amazon.com has an arrangement to take self-published titles.

Again, self-publishing is a lot of work, but if you've got the energy, this route can prove highly successful. And keep in mind that many self-published books wind up getting picked up by big publishers, often for very large advances.

For an overview of the entire self-publishing process, visit the Web site of self-publishing guru Dan Poynter at www .parapublishing.com.

> **HELPFUL HINT:** If you self-publish, it's probably a bad idea to edit yourself. You need someone who can look at your novel objectively—preferably a professional editor and not a friend or relative.

Print-on-Demand

Don't want a garage full of books? Then you may want to consider print-on-demand publishing, or POD. Using a new technology that allows the printing and binding of a small

number of books in only a few minutes, this method eliminates the need for print runs in the thousands, which in turn
eliminates the problem of storing large numbers of unsold
books.

Nearly all POD books are manufactured in trade (quality)
paperback format; a few are published in hardcover. Because of economies of scale, price per copy is liable to be higher
than one would normally expect for a trade paperback (often as high as $25 or $30), but the quality is typically quite
good. Most POD books are attractive and professionally
designed.

There are basically two types of POD publishers:

Fee-Based POD Services

iUniverse and Xlibris are two examples of fee-based POD services. As the name implies, fee-based POD services charge
authors a setup fee ranging from $99 to more than $1,000 for
publication, then pay royalties on books sold. These royalties are usually net royalties (based on the publisher's receipts
rather than on the book's cover price).

Fee-based POD services do not screen books for publication; anyone willing to pay the fee is eligible. The good
news, then, is that anyone can get published. The bad news is
that anyone can get published. Poorly written novels appear alongside well-written ones, which makes some readers
and reviewers wary.

These companies make their books available to consumers
through their Web sites, as well as through Amazon and
other online booksellers. They also have their books listed in
the catalogues of the major book distributors such as In-

gram, Baker & Taylor, and Brodart, so that the books may be ordered by bookstores and libraries.

If you decide to work with a fee-based print-on-demand publisher, make sure you know exactly what you'll be getting for your fee. Some fee-based POD publishers that charge higher fees include media kits or marketing packages. If you work with one of these companies, find out what will be included in these kits or packages.

Ask if there might be additional fees later. For example, you might receive an invoice for cover design, or for obtaining an ISBN or registering copyright.

Before you sign with one of these companies, get in touch with others who have already used the service to see if they are satisfied.

POD-Based Publishers

POD-based publishers are simply publishers that use print-on-demand technology exclusively to manufacture their books. Unlike fee-based POD services, these companies screen submissions like traditional publishers. They don't ask authors for fees, but they usually do not pay advances, either. An advance, if there is one, usually averages only a few hundred dollars.

If you are offered a contract by a POD-based publisher, order a few of its titles. Are they well written? Are the books themselves well designed and attractive, with few or no errors?

As with fee-based POD services, contact writers who have been published by this company and find out if they are satisfied.

You'll find a list of selected POD publishers on the Internet at a Web site called Published.com. Go to www.published.com/forum/booklink.html.

Cooperative Publishers

For those who like the idea of self-publishing but find the undertaking too daunting, there are cooperative publishers. These are publishers that ask the author to foot some of the cost of producing the book. (Don't confuse this with subsidy or vanity publishing, in which the author pays the *entire* cost, as well as a healthy markup that goes right into the publisher's pocket.) Some subsidy publishers ask the author to contribute by supplying camera-ready copy, which means you have to take care of the editing, copyediting, and typesetting, or pay others to handle these functions for you.

You'll find that some smaller publishers produce books all three ways: traditional commercial publishing, cooperative publishing, and subsidy publishing. If you work with one of these outfits, make sure you know which kind of deal you're getting yourself into.

Electronic Publishing

"Cyberpublishing" is the newest form of self-publishing. Companies seem to spring up daily, publishing books in various electronic formats. Some e-books are for hardware readers—dedicated devices for the sole purpose of reading these cyberbooks. Others are for software readers—computer programs that allow you to read electronic books on your monitor's screen. Or you can order a floppy disk to pop into your computer.

As you may have guessed, this new form of publishing is still sorting itself out. The possibilities are exciting for writers who, for whatever reason, have been unsuccessful in gaining the attention of the large traditional print publishers (which tend to avoid risk), or who have, for whatever reason, not bothered trying.

If you decide to explore this route, be careful. There are excellent, reputable companies, and there are companies that promise royalties but never pay them due to hidden charges.

For a comprehensive overview of this new technology, as well as listings of e-publishers, I recommend *Writer's Online Marketplace*, by Debbie Ridpath Ohi (Writer's Digest Books).

The Contract

Much about the contracts from these alternative publishers will be the same as in traditional publishers' contracts, which means you can follow many of the guidelines in chapter eighteen.

Some alternative publishers display their contracts on their Web sites. If a publisher you're investigating does this, print out the contract and study it, marking points you don't understand or don't like, so you'll be ready to negotiate if you and this company make a deal.

The most important points in the contract are the royalties and the period of time the contract covers. Royalties typically run up to 50 percent of receipts. Some publishers may stagger the royalties, starting at a lower rate—say, 25 percent—and increasing in stages to 50 percent.

A contract will usually cover one year, with an option to renew at the end of this period. Make sure there's a provision for termination.

No matter which alternate publishing route you choose,

your contract will be extensive and probably complicated. Make sure you understand everything above your signature; if necessary, hire a lawyer familiar with publishing to explain or negotiate clauses you don't like.

If you choose a reputable company with good references that produces quality work, there's no reason why publishing your book by one of the above methods can't be a fun and gratifying experience.

Best of all, you'll be published. Your book will be in a form that can be shared with the rest of the world. Your words will be providing pleasure and entertainment to others.

And that's why you started writing a novel in the first place, right?

To your success!

CHAPTER 21

You're Just Getting Started: The Secrets of Dogged Persistence, Longevity, and Adaptability

Congratulations! Your novel is published, your family and friends are complimenting you on the great read, and the hard work is over, right?

Wrong! You want a writing *career*, right? You're not just a one-hit wonder. If at all possible, you'd like to be doing this for a while. Then here are some points to consider:

Never Stop Learning

If you want to gain a loyal and growing following, you're going to have to keep your readers happy. The way to do this is to keep supplying them with top-quality entertainment—and to keep topping yourself. If you don't improve—don't continue to try to exceed your last effort—your readers will grow bored and move on to other writers. You can't let that happen.

How do you keep improving? For one thing, you keep writing. Some techniques and abilities are discovered only in the actual act of writing. So always keep writing, not only because you're going to need book after book to sell, but because the act of writing makes you a better writer.

> **HELPFUL HINT:** Want to keep your mind nimble? Try writing short stories in your genre. The short story is a discipline of its own that will exercise your brain in a whole new way. Who knows—you may discover a whole new area of writing that you enjoy. Read magazines and fanzines; see if they publish short fiction; write or e-mail for submission guidelines, or check their Web sites.

You may want to join a critique group. These are small groups of writers, often with similar interests, who read and honestly critique one another's work. Be careful, though. A critique group made up mostly of unpublished writers may be of no use to you at all. Check the credentials of a critique group's members before you join.

> **HELPFUL HINT:** If you join or start a critique group, members should agree on a set of ground rules for the critiquing itself. Rules can ensure that the criticism is helpful, positive, and constructive, and can help to keep personal matters out.

Attend writers conferences and conventions. There you'll not only enjoy the company of other writers, but you'll also gain exposure and learn about what's being written in your genre.

Read periodicals about books, such as *The New York Times Book Review* or *The New York Review of Books*, and specialized fanzines geared toward your interests, such as *Romantic Times Book Club* and *Locus*.

Keep haunting bookstores. Attend readings and book signings, especially if the author writes in your genre.

In other words, keep yourself immersed in the world of books.

Promote

Do what your time and budget allow in terms of self-promotion. The days of just writing the novel and then sitting back and letting the publisher do the rest are over. At the very least, have book signings in your area, and send postcards notifying family and friends when your novel is published. If you have the inclination, become more innovative and aggressive in your promotion efforts. Stage local events tied to elements in your novel and invite the media. Hold competitions on your Web site. Mail clever promotional items to bookstores.

Self-promotion not only helps you sell more books; it also increases your value to your publisher.

Adapt

Reading tastes seem to be changing faster than ever before. If you keep writing exactly the same kind of book, without regard for these changes, you may be writing yourself into obsolescence. When you spot a new trend, read a book or two that exemplify the trend, if only to stay aware of what's being published. Who knows—you might want to try your hand at it yourself.

Eventually, you're going to have to change in some way. Many artists have survived for decades because they are so good at reinventing themselves: think singer-actress Cher. You may have to reinvent your writing to stay successful.

I have represented writers who landed six-figure contracts at the height of their careers. Twenty years later I can't give their books away. Why? Because those writers were caught in a literary time trap; they were neither aware of nor cared about how tastes were changing. Yet others who suffered this fate were victims of their own egos. *Why,* they asked, *should I change how I write, when at one time I was so successful? The fans are still out there.* No, they're not. They have grown tired of reading the same book over and over, while the world continues to change. They have moved on to writers who have kept pace with the world.

Keep Reading

This one's a no-brainer. Of course you'll keep reading, first and foremost because you love it. What writer doesn't love to read?

Then why am I even bothering to suggest it? Because many writers become so busy writing that they stop reading. To do this is to close yourself off not only from what your own fans are buying, but, more importantly, from the competition. You've got to know what you're up against. You've also got to know what kinds of stories are being written, or else a novel you've got in mind that you think is fresh and different may actually be trite and overdone. See Helpful Hint on next page.

Understand the Ups and Downs

This one is difficult. It involves understanding and accepting that very few writers rise steadily to the top and stay there.

HELPFUL HINT: Once in a while, read something completely outside your chosen genre. If you write cozy mysteries, read a horror novel. If you write literary fiction, read a commercial thriller. Good writing is good writing, and we can all learn from one another. Reading outside your genre expands and refreshes your thinking. You'll also find yourself borrowing the most effective techniques from other genres and thus improving your writing.

Usually a writer will rise and fall, or perhaps rise, stay there awhile, and then fall. By "fall," I don't mean that his books do not sell, though that can happen. More often, a writer's sales drop, so his advances follow suit.

Publishing is a difficult industry—more profit-oriented than ever before. This is no longer a gentleman's business, so develop that rhinoceros hide I mentioned earlier. If your material is rejected (and you *will* get rejected from time to time, even after you've made that first sale), forget it and move on. If you are offered a lower advance than you received for your last book because your sales have dropped, resolve to write a better book that will cause your sales to rise again. Redouble your promotion efforts. You're a writer, right? In good times and bad, large advances and small, you must keep writing. You never know—your twentieth book might be the one that hits national best-seller lists. It happens all the time. I'll guarantee you one thing, though: Stop writing and your chances of hitting any list at all are zero.

It doesn't matter, though, because you're not going to stop

writing. You're a writer. Writers write. They can't *not* write. So whether it's your twentieth book that makes those national best-seller lists or your fortieth—or whether you never make those lists at all—what's the difference?

I can't stop, and I know you won't either.

Writing is in our blood. It's how we relate to the world. If we stop doing it, we suffer withdrawal symptoms. Besides, there are people out there who (though they don't know it yet) are waiting to be moved, educated, and most of all, entertained by your novels.

Don't let them down.

Marshall Planner: Career Dream Roadmap

No, the device on the following page isn't Candyland or Monopoly; it's the Marshall Planner: Career Dream Roadmap, a handy tool to help you plan your writing career, depending upon the kinds of novels you write. As with the other Marshall Planners, I recommend that you photocopy the Roadmap before you use it. As you progress in your career, your writing interests may change, and you may want to use this tool again to chart a new course.

You may find it helpful to trace your path with a Highlighter as you travel downward on the Roadmap. Then post the Planner someplace where it's always in sight, so that your goals are clearly before you.

Marshall Planner: Career Dream Roadmap

START HERE ▼

Before you embark on your journey, define the novel you have written or are writing. Be as objective as you can. *My novel is...*

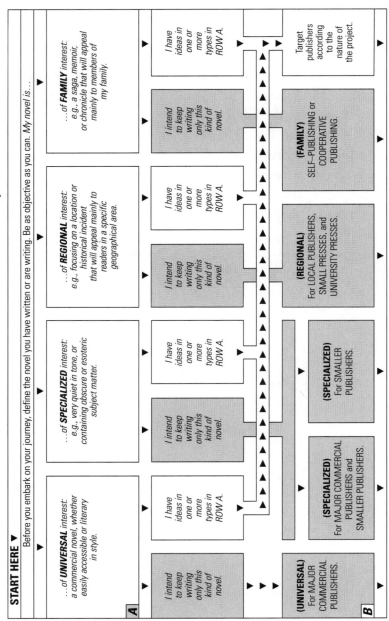

...of **UNIVERSAL** interest: a commercial novel, whether easily accessible or literary in style.

...of **SPECIALIZED** interest: e.g., very quiet in tone, or containing obscure or esoteric subject matter.

...of **REGIONAL** interest: e.g., focusing on a location or historical incident that will appeal mainly to readers in a specific geographical area.

...of **FAMILY** interest: e.g., a saga, memoir, or chronicle that will appeal mainly to members of my family.

A

I intend to keep writing only this kind of novel.

I have ideas in one or more types in ROW A.

(UNIVERSAL) For MAJOR COMMERCIAL PUBLISHERS.

(SPECIALIZED) For MAJOR COMMERCIAL PUBLISHERS and SMALLER PUBLISHERS.

(SPECIALIZED) For SMALLER PUBLISHERS.

(REGIONAL) For LOCAL PUBLISHERS, SMALL PRESSES, and UNIVERSITY PRESSES.

(FAMILY) SELF-PUBLISHING or COOPERATIVE PUBLISHING.

Target publishers according to the nature of the project.

B

You need an agent. Query agents and editors simul-taneously. If you get an offer and still don't have an agent, bring one in to handle your deal.

You'd probably benefit from having an agent. Query agents and editors simultaneously. Bring in an agent if you get an offer from a major publisher.

You don't necessarily need an agent. Query agents and editors simultaneously.

You won't need an agent; these publishers are used to working directly with authors.

You won't need an agent; these publishers are used to working directly with authors.

You may need an agent for some of your novels, but not for others.

When novel is published, work with your publisher to aggressively promote the book.

When novel is published, work with your publisher to aggressively promote the book.

When novel is published, ask local bookstores to sell copies.

When novel is published, ask local bookstores to sell copies.

For each project, go to ROW B above, find your novel's category, and then follow the *shaded* route downward

REMEMBER, to succeed in this area, you must be:
• RESILIENT
• ADAPTABLE
• PROLIFIC (at least a book a year)

Promote to regional media such as radio, TV, and newspapers.

Write more of these novels as they occur to you.

211

Glossary of Marshall Plan Terms

In this glossary you'll find definitions of important terms used in my Marshall Plan system of novel writing. Words set in italics are defined in the glossary. To learn more about these terms, see *The Marshall Plan for Novel Writing* and *The Marshall Plan Workbook*.

Action writing mode. A manner of fiction writing in which every action is dramatized chronologically with no summary.

Action section. A *section* in which a character pursues a *section goal* he believes will help him achieve the *story goal*.

Background writing mode. A manner of fiction writing in which background information is presented.

Beginning. The first quarter of the novel, in which the *lead* character experiences the *crisis* and sets his *story goal*, all characters are introduced, and all background information is presented.

Character fact list. A compilation of basic facts about a character, necessary to establish before plotting the novel.

Confidant. A character who serves as an advisor to and sounding board for the *lead*.

Connector. A device for connecting one *section* with the next. The three types of connectors are the *space-break connector*, *run-together connector*, and *summary connector*.

Crisis. A disastrous event that forces the *lead* to set a *story goal* of restoring his or her life to normal.

Crisis criteria. Conditions a *crisis* must satisfy to work effectively in a novel. There are three crisis criteria: (1) The *crisis* must be genre-appropriate, (2) it must turn the *lead*'s life upside down in a negative way, and (3) it must capture the writer's imagination.

Dialogue writing mode. A manner of fiction writing in which dialogue is of central importance.

End. The last quarter of the novel, in which all *story lines* are resolved, the *lead* finally vanquishing the *opposition* and achieving the *story goal*.

External conflict. A situation or circumstance that stands in the way of two characters' entering into a romantic relationship.

Feelings/thoughts writing mode. A manner of fiction writing in which a character's feelings and thoughts are presented.

Flashback. Past story action presented as its own full-fledged *action section*.

Genre. A category of fiction, such as horror, romance, or mystery. Your target genre is the type of novel in which you have decided to specialize.

Internal conflict. An emotional resistance within a character that makes him reluctant to commit to a romantic relationship.

Lead. A novel's main character: its hero or heroine. A novel is first and foremost about the lead's pursuit of his or her *story goal*.

Lead's subplot. A *story line*, secondary to the *main story line*, in which the *lead* pursues a separate goal.

Line. A publisher's program of novels of a particular *genre*; for example, a line of romances or Westerns.

Main story line. The *lead*'s pursuit of the *story goal*.

Middle. The central portion of the novel, constituting half its length. In the middle, the principal action of the *lead*'s pursuit of the *story goal* takes place.

Opposition. The character who most stands in the way of the *lead*'s achieving his *story goal*.

Point of hopelessness. The *lead*'s darkest moment, directly following the *worst failure*, when it appears he has failed to achieve the *story goal* and all hope is lost.

Reaction section. A *section* in which a character responds to what happened in his previous *action section*.

Romantic involvement. A character who is the object of the *lead*'s romantic and/or sexual interest.

Run-together connector. A *section*-joining device consisting of running one *section* right from the last, with no break in the text other than the start of a new paragraph.

Saving act. A heroic action the *lead* takes to defeat the *opposition* and achieve the *story goal*.

Section. A single unit of story action in the novel. A section can be an *action section* or a *reaction section*.

Section character. The focal character of a *section*, from whose viewpoint the *section* is planned and written.

Section goal. The short-term goal (toward the *story goal*) a character pursues within a single *action section*.

Section sheet. A template on which you plan what will happen in a *section*.

Space-break connector. A *section*-joining device consisting of a blank line or space containing a centered asterisk between sections.

Story goal. The objective a character pursues throughout the novel to solve the *crisis*.

Story goal criteria. Conditions a *lead*'s *story goal* must satisfy. There are four story goal criteria: (1) The *lead* must seek possession of or relief from something, (2) he must face terrible consequences if he fails to achieve the *story goal*, (3) he must have a worthy motivation for pursuing the *story goal*, and (4) he must face tremendous odds in pursuing the *story goal*.

Story idea. The *lead*'s *suppose* (*crisis*) combined with his *story goal*.

Story line. A distinct plot thread in which a character pursues a goal.

Subplot. See *story line*.

Summary connector. A *section*-joining device consisting of a paragraph or two of summarized action.

Summary writing mode. A manner of fiction writing in which story action is presented in a condensed, narrative form.

Suppose. An idea for a *crisis* for a novel's *lead*.

Surprise. A shocking development in the *lead*'s *main story line*. A novel has three surprises: (1) at the end of the *beginning*, (2) at the novel's midpoint, and (3) at the end of the *middle*.

Synopsis. A brief narrative summary of a novel.

Tip sheet. A publisher's guidelines to writing for a specific *line* of books.

Viewpoint character. The character through whose perceptions and awareness a *section* is planned and written.

Viewpoint writing. A method of writing in which everything is filtered through the perceptions and awareness of a specific *viewpoint character*.

Word length. The customary length of a given type of novel, expressed in the number of words, usually rounded to the nearest 10,000.

Worst failure. The ultimate confrontation between the *lead* and the *opposition*, in which the *lead* utterly fails (see *point of hopelessness*).

Wrap-up. The novel's final *section*, following the *lead*'s attainment of the *story goal*, in which we see him restored to a state of happiness.

Sample Query Letters

The first query letter on the next page was written by Jerrilyn Farmer, a client of my agency. I was impressed by her credentials, and her humor made me laugh. Most important, the story sounded like something I could probably sell. So I asked to see it.

You'll notice that the letter differs somewhat from the structure presented in chapter eleven. That's okay; it's all there, in a pleasing arrangement. When you know the rules, it's all right to judiciously break them.

November 6, 1995

Evan Marshall
The Evan Marshall Agency
Six Tristam Place
Pine Brook, NJ 07058

Dear Evan Marshall:

I've spent thirteen years writing for television, and in the process of earning those welcome residuals, a less-welcome stomach condition, and a couple of CableAce Awards, I have met a colorful assortment of low-lifes with money and high-flyers without. They deserve to be exposed, some even prosecuted and convicted. But, what with the whimsical nature of our justice system, I felt fiction was the only court left that could be relied upon for true justice.

In SYMPATHY FOR THE DEVIL, a temperamental television producer hosts an extravagant Hollywood party on Halloween night, spending over a quarter of a million dollars to make the night ''memorable.'' It's memorable all right. For murder. When the clever young caterer, Madeline Bean, finds her

continued

partner becoming the prime suspect, she begins to
unravel a mystery that leads her back to the early
days of California's land grants. A long forgotten
dirty deal inspired a nineteenth-century Spanish
curse that may still haunt the plush, historic Los
Feliz neighborhood to this day.

Perhaps. But Madeline, wit intact, manages to bring
things bumping back to the present. In the process,
she uncovers a bizarre scheme of sperm fraud, a pair
of vicious pit bulls named Nancy and Hillary, and
a trail of offbeat '90s characters, one of whom must
certainly have decided a little strychnine would
spice up the death of rich and loathsome Bruno
Huntley.

SYMPATHY FOR THE DEVIL is an amateur sleuth novel
of approximately 85,000 words. I am currently
working full-time on the second Madeline Bean mystery in the series.

In addition to a personal acquaintance with many of
Hollywood's scoundrels and sirens, I've spent years
writing a food-centered television series which
provides background for my protagonist's working life as a gourmet chef. I've studied mystery
writing with Melodie Johnson Howe at the UCLA

Writers Program, and meet with an active writers
group, and I believe my manuscript is ready for
the world. I would be delighted to send it to you
with the hope that you might be interested in representing it.

Best wishes,

Jerrilyn Farmer

The next sample query letter was written by another client
of my agency, Laura Levine. She took a more traditional
approach, but her letter contained all the right elements and,
like Jerrilyn Farmer's letter, sent a message of professional-
ism. Note that Ms. Levine included her résumé, which was
helpful because it detailed the TV credits she refers to in
the letter.

Ms. Levine's letter intrigued me, and I immediately asked
to see her manuscript, which in turn made me laugh out loud—
and offer her representation. Almost immediately I got her
a three-book contract with John Scognamiglio, an Editorial Director at Kensington Publishing. As of this writing,
Ms. Levine has published *This Pen for Hire* and has her
second Jaine Austen mystery, *Last Writes*, coming out in a
few months. She's currently at work on the last book of
her contract and will be ready for a new contract soon.

November 13, 2000

Evan Marshall
The Evan Marshall Agency
Six Tristam Place
Pine Brook, NJ 07058

Dear Mr. Marshall:

I'm writing to see if you'd be interested in representing a book I've written.

As you can see from my résumé, I've got lots of professional writing experience. I've had a successful career as a sitcom writer, with more than 65 produced episodes to my credit (one of which was named one of *TV Guide*'s ''Hundred Greatest Episodes of All Time'').

I've also been published twice before: One was a humor book; the other a young adult novel. And I am currently writing comedy material for Garrison Keillor's ''A Prairie Home Companion.''

My book is a murder mystery called THIS PEN FOR HIRE, about a freelance writer who (just barely) makes a living writing résumés and letters and any

other writing gig she can drum up. One day a painfully shy guy shows up at her doorstep. He wants
her to write a love letter to a beautiful woman he's
admired from afar but never actually spoken to.
Reluctantly, she takes the job. She writes the letter, hoping it will get him a date. Never dreaming
it will get him arrested for murder.

If you'd like to see my manuscript (or just a few
chapters), I'd be happy to send it to you.

Sincerely,

Laura Levine

Sample Cover Letter

Jerrilyn Farmer's manuscript arrived about a week after I requested it, accompanied by the excellent and rather clever cover letter below.

December 19, 1995

Evan Marshall
The Evan Marshall Agency
Six Tristam Place
Pine Brook, NJ 07058

Dear Evan Marshall:

Needless to say, I was delighted to receive your letter requesting the manuscript of SYMPATHY FOR THE DEVIL, a mystery that spices a stew of lavish Hollywood lifestyles with a dash of strychnine.

Featuring gourmet cooking, a true-life crime from early California history, a devil of a producer whom everyone seems glad to see drop painfully dead, a soothsayer and a loan shark, I like to say there's something here for just about anyone.

I picture you, the image of a successful but kind literary agent, seated by the window in an old leather wing chair. Snow is falling outside. I can almost see you sipping eggnog and turning to page one of SYMPATHY FOR THE DEVIL. (We fantasize a lot in L.A.)

Happy holidays. I look forward to hearing from you. And thanks, once again, for your interest in my writing.

Sincerely,

Jerrilyn Farmer

As it happens, I loathe eggnog. But how could I resist? Seriously, though, Jerrilyn Farmer's letters radiated vibes of a person of wit, humor, and sanity—that last one counts for a lot in publishing. Of course, the proof of the pudding was the manuscript itself, which, happily, was delightful and highly salable. I offered to represent Ms. Farmer immediately.

Avon Books Senior Editor Lyssa Keusch liked Ms. Farmer's work as much as I did, and offered her a three-book contract. After *Sympathy for the Devil*, Ms. Farmer published *Immaculate Reception*, *Killer Wedding*, and *Dim Sum Dead*, all to rave reviews and ever-increasing sales. As of this writing, her next Madeline Bean novel, *Mumbo Gumbo*, is in production as a William Morrow hardcover. Jerrilyn's future looks very bright indeed, and it all started with a cleverly written query letter.

Sample Long Synopsis

Evelyn Rogers, also a client of my agency, is a veteran and beloved writer of romances who has recently been dubbed the Queen of the Modern Gothic. Not only does she write wonderful novels; she also has a masterful way with synopses. On the next page, for example, is the synopsis for one of her recent novels, a Gothic titled *The Grotto*, which was published by Dorchester Publishing.

Notice how quickly and smoothly Ms. Rogers sets up the lead, her crisis, and the story goal—all in the first paragraph, which also serves as an intriguing hook.

Evelyn Rogers   Historical Romance

c/o The Evan Marshall Agency   100,000 words

Six Tristam Place   Synopsis

Pine Brook, NJ 07058

THE GROTTO

After the drowning death of her debauched Italian no-
bleman husband, American-born CONTESSA CATERINA
DONATI retires to the only home creditors have left
her, an abandoned Tuscan villa known as Il Falcone.
Once grand, Falcone long ago fell into disrepair following a curse laid upon a past generation. With no
family left in her native country and her fortune
squandered by the late conte, Kate has no choice but
to attempt a revival of the parched olive grove and
vineyard that are a part of the estate.

  Her first day in residence, while examining the
overgrown vineyard, she sees in shadow a vine
looped over the branch of a gnarled, leafless tree,
her own shadow seemingly hanging from the vine as
if it were a noose. Suddenly the shadow of a man
looms beside her. She screams and bolts forward,
terrified by the fancy that this newcomer is her executioner. Falling, she stares up at the most handsome man she has ever seen, despite his rude cloth-
ing, a dark man with classic features and
penetrating eyes. He extends a hand; reluctantly

she takes it, feeling foolish yet unable to shake the fear that has taken hold of her.

He introduces himself as ROBERTO TORELLI, a worker newly come to the seaside village that lies at the base of Falcone. He has not found employment and offers to help with the vineyard, taking his pay from the profit he is sure will result, scoffing at the curse that the villagers believe brings doom to all who walk Donati land.

Telling herself her fears are as foolish as her attraction to his powerful presence, she reluctantly agrees. Long pampered though otherwise ignored by her adulterous husband, considered weak because of her look of fair-haired frailty, she gladly throws herself into the hard work of clearing the land of dead growth, turning the soil, cleaning the many rooms, the courtyard, and the statuary-lined terrace of the villa, frequently staring at the Mediterranean, growing strong as she works, thinking of the far-away land that had once been her home until her ambitious father gave her to her titled husband.

Always at her side is Roberto, helpful, courteous, never forward, yet she senses in him a smoldering interest in her and a desire for more than an occasional brush of hands. Within her burns an

continued

equal desire. Lonely most of her life, patronized
by both her father and husband, she wonders what
the comfort of a man's arms and the warmth of his
kisses would be like.

The work does not go well, as much from the drought
as from a series of accidents that befall her. One
night she sees a shadowy figure on the terrace and
fancifully thinks it is a statue come to life. But
no, the figure is all too human. Grabbing a lamp, she
hurries down to investigate. The figure scurries
into the darkness along a twisting trail and Kate,
armed with a pistol that had been her husband's,
follows. Intent on the chase, she falls into an unseen gaping fissure, the lamp and gun instantly
lost, her body descending rapidly down a sloping tunnel, scraping against the narrow walls which slow
her descent. She lands in the dark on what seems to be
a makeshift bed. Hovering close to unconscious-
ness, she is awakened by gentle hands and a deep,
soothing voice she recognizes as Roberto's.

It takes a minute to realize he is speaking to her
in English as his hands roam over her body, looking,
he assures her, for broken bones. The search is thorough; she does not protest and soon she is nestled
in his arms, enjoying the sweet kisses he brushes
across her lips, scarcely aware of crashing waves
outside the grotto into which she has fallen.

Sanity slowly returns and she pushes away. In answer to her questions about his knowledge of English, he explains that as a boy he ran away to sea and lived awhile in London. But it was never his home. He has returned to Tuscany, intent on renewing the life for which he was born. An uncharacteristic sharpness in his voice startles her and she is once again reminded of her first image of him as her executioner. She shakes off the thought, telling herself she has just suffered an almost fatal accident and is not thinking clearly.

It matters not that the troubles at the villa have increased her dependency on him. He surely could not be the source of these troubles. It is the curse, which fell on the land when an ancestor of the conte was slashed and scarred by a falcon belonging to a member of the wealthy and powerful Medici family. In a drunken rage, he slew the bird and the curse fell on the land and the Donati descendants.

One result of the curse, Roberto now tells her, was a deadly storm that sent the sea flooding into the grotto, washing away the crates of vintage wine that had been stored within, drowning two workers who tried to save the crates. Lifting the lamp he has brought, she stares into the depths of the grotto, then to the blanket-covered mattress upon

continued

which she fell. He puts off her questions about who might be its owner, instead cradling her in his arms for the perilous journey through the mouth of the cave, along a rocky path to the nearby village, then upward on horseback to the safety of the villa.

In the ensuing days, she finds herself drawn to Roberto even more and soon they become lovers. STEFANO BRAGGIO, her agent in Florence, visits and warns her to be wary of a man so far below her, declaring he has had reports of her ongoing troubles, begging her to let him sell the villa and settle her in the growing Florentine exile community of English and Americans. Against her wishes, he takes residence in the village, swearing to protect her as her husband the conte would have wanted.

After a visit to him, she comes across Roberto talking in heated anger with a beautiful signorina, his hands falling on her shoulders, her hands rubbing against the sleeves of his shirt. The words come too fast for Kate to interpret little more than the woman's name, ELENA, but it is obvious much passion is involved. She drops away, unseen, but she is heart sore. Roberto had told her his people were gone from the area, that there was no one he knew from the early years in Tuscany.

Later, sensing her troubled spirit, he kisses away her doubts and she responds with an urgency that takes them both by surprise.

A week later, when Kate goes to the village for supplies, Elena approaches her with a warning to be careful of Roberto, prophesying that he will bring about her doom. "He is like the falcon," she hisses, "an assassin in his world, willing to do what must be done to get what he wants. The curse falls on you, too, Contessa Donati."

Giving Kate no chance to reply, she disappears into the crowded village street. Shaken, Kate wanders away from the village and along the rocky coastline—searching, she realizes, for the grotto into which she had fallen. Its interior lighted by the bright afternoon sun, the grotto beckons. Perhaps she can find the answer to a question she has long held at bay: How did Roberto find her so quickly? He must have been in the grotto, or close to it. Why?

Deep in the interior she finds a high-ceilinged room with what appear to be remnants of ruined wine crates at the rear. Nearby are signs of a recent fire, close to the mattress upon which she had fallen. It is as though she has stumbled upon someone's private quarters. Suddenly frightened, she turns

continued

and runs into Roberto's broad chest, feels his hands sharply clutching her arms.

Furious, he questions her presence in such a dangerous place. She tells him she could question the same of him. Smugglers and thieves have been known to inhabit the grotto, he declares, adding that she has too soon forgotten how the stormy sea can bring death to those who seek safety there. What has that to do with her? she asks. Surely he does not mean that he is a danger to her. Besides, the only storm she knows of is the anger that now thunders between them. In the dim light, with the rhythm of the sea echoing around them, their anger turns to lust and they make love.

It is only later Kate realizes that once again he has given no reason for his presence in the grotto. But she is so devoured by her love for him, she pushes aside any further questions. Even when she sees him talking furtively to her agent Signor Braggio, she tells herself they speak only of her welfare. Braggio contradicts her belief, saying Roberto Torelli has asked pointed questions concerning the terms of her inheritance, wanting especially to know what would happen should she remarry.

Before Kate can confront Roberto with Braggio's revelations, Elena appears on the terrace, and Kate realizes it was she who led her on the wild

chase that culminated in her fall. The air thick and
heavy with promise of a storm and lightning flash-
ing in the distance, Elena says that Roberto has returned to Tuscany to claim land that is rightfully
his, that he will get it however he can, even if he
has to marry the foreigner who has invaded his
home. "I warned you he would be your doom. He mar-
ries you, then you die, and he is free to marry the
woman he truly loves."

Her smile of evil triumph says louder than words
that she is that woman.

She has saved one last knife to stab at Kate's
wounded heart: "Do you not recognize him? He is
the conte's brother, the last true heir of the Do-
natis. Ask him if you dare. He awaits in our secret
hiding place." Kate realizes she means the grotto.

Elena leads her to the fissure, showing her the
narrow steps she missed on her fall, then starts
her on her way as the storm breaks. The fury Kate
hears echoing down the stairway tunnel is nothing
beside the torment raging inside her. Everything
the woman revealed rings true, especially Roberto's identity. He had in truth looked familiar to
her, but his demeanor was so different from the
late conte's, she had not made the connection.

Dropping onto the mattress, she gives way to
continued

tears, crying herself into a state of exhaustion as
she listens to the storm, in the dark unaware of the
waves lapping onto the grotto's stony floor, unaware
of the passage of time. Voices from the direction
of the tunnel stairway stir her to alertness. Dimly
she recognizes her lover and the woman he truly
loves. Struggling to her feet, she presses her back
against the rough stone wall as Roberto, lamp in
hand, and Elena appear, still arguing.

Setting the lamp aside, he hurries toward her.
With a scream, Elena throws herself at him and the
two fall into fast-rising water at the edge of the
grotto floor, sinking into its inky depths. Horrified, Kate stares at the roiling surface, fighting to keep from throwing herself after them.
After an eternity, Roberto appears, pulling himself out of the water, his eyes wild in the dim
light. Did he drown Elena? Did he try to save her?
Her thoughts in chaos, Kate is barely aware of the
water lapping at her feet, soaking the hem of her
gown. "Out!" Roberto roars over the storm, and
she stumbles toward the tunnel, pulling herself up
the stairs, expecting him to follow.

But he does not and she hurries through the rain
toward the beckoning light of the villa. On the
terrace, a dark figure appears. Braggio grabs her
arm, declaring she is a fool as he drags her

inside. As if suddenly aware of his roughness, he
assumes his sycophantic air, telling her he wor-
ries for her safety. But Kate can think only of her
lover, gone with Elena. Pain engulfs her. Braggio
puts a comforting arm around her as Roberto appears
and orders the agent to let her go. But he tightens
his hold, rasping that she must be protected from
the scoundrel who would marry her and take her
land. Pulling free, Kate asks if what the agent
claims is true, saying it is no more than Elena has
already revealed, including the accusation that
Roberto is her late husband's half brother.

Roberto admits that having heard in England of the
contessa's bereft state, he returned to Tuscany to
take her as his wife, the only way he could claim the
land he viewed as his though his mother was a lowly
servant in the villa. But he had not planned to fall
in love with her, wanting her no matter her name or
position, trapped by his scheme, unable to tell her
of his feelings. Braggio interrupts and Kate backs
away from both men as they hurl accusations at one another, Roberto accusing the agent of wanting to
sell the Donati properties at a great profit to himself, setting up the so-called accidents that have
threatened the contessa with ruin, using the story
of the curse as his cover.

continued

Without warning, the agent pulls a pistol on Roberto, saying he will kill him as honor dictates
for such scurrilous lies. Horror-stricken, knowing only that she cannot live without love, Kate
throws herself at Braggio. Roberto tries to push
her aside and in the ensuing scuffle the pistol
discharges and the agent falls dead.

Later, after the GRAND DUKE'S constables have
come and gone, Roberto confesses all: His mother gave
birth to him in the grotto, then threw herself into
the water and drowned. Her infant was found by
Elena's family, who raised him, always letting him
know of his disgraceful state. When still a boy he
ran away to sea, eventually finding his way onto an
English ship, then on to London. From the beginning Elena had attached herself to him and assumed
his return was for her. Her death by drowning in
the same water that took his mother was a terrible
blow and he tried to find her in the rising water,
but to no avail.

The grotto has always had a special hold on him.
The bedding was his, providing a bit of comfort in
the stolen hours he spent in the secret confines of
the cave. Beginning with the first near-fatal
fall, Elena had directed Kate there, hoping her ri-
val would begin to learn the truth, fearful for a
while of telling her outright and earning Rober-

to's wrath. But with the night storm and the latest
tragedy, the hold is gone. He needs light as much as
he needs love.

As Kate stands quietly at the edge of the terrace,
watching the storm clouds blow away in the distance, he declares he has one more truth to reveal:
In England he made his fortune, returning to Tuscany a wealthier man than the conte had ever been.
This fortune he pledges to Caterina, if she will
have him. He also apologizes for allowing her to
toil so hard when he could have hired workers to
clear the vineyard and repair the villa.

Kate hushes him with fingers pressed to his lips,
saying that all her life she had been cared for, pampered and ignored. True happiness has come through
hard labor, where she can see tangible results of
her own efforts, can feel good about herself for the
first time. Most important of all, Roberto has
been at her side, encouraging her, teaching her
about how much she can achieve. It hasn't hurt,
she adds with a smile, that he has taught her the
meaning of true passion. She loves him, and it matters
not who or what he is.

As the morning sun breaks through the clouds and
a falcon swoops high over the cypress-lined hills
of Tuscany, they swear their love, knowing at last
that the Donati curse is broken.

Sample Short Synopsis

Here is Jerrilyn Farmer's short synopsis for her fifth Madeline Bean mystery, *Mumbo Gumbo*.

Jerrilyn Farmer
c/o Evan Marshall
The Evan Marshall Agency
Six Tristam Place
Pine Brook, NJ 07058-9445

Mystery
80,000 words
Synopsis

MUMBO GUMBO

When celebrity chef SEBASTIAN PLUME, the insane host of America's favorite new game show, *Shoot the Chef*, wants to celebrate the completion of his first fabulous season, he calls Mad Bean Events to create a wrap party no one will forget. The entire cast and crew of the series, as well as Madeline's

producer friend, DARA OLIVER, attend the lavish af-
fair, which is held after-hours at the Beverly
Hills Gun Range. Needless to say, they are all having a blast.

But on that festive night there's more to shoot
than just the breeze: A practice gun is aimed at a
live target. A man is shot.

Amid the chaos of that firearms ''accident,''
news comes that the network has just ordered four
more weeks of episodes! What joy! So, forgetting
for a moment the unpleasantness of the gunshot
mishap (''Well, after all, it isn't as if the guy is
actually *dead* . . . yet''), all those revelers
who've been on the verge of unemployment instead
drink toasts to their month-long reprieve. All,
that is, except BRADLEY DART, one of the show's culinary question writers. It seems Brad ducked out
of the party rather too early and is not expected
back anytime soon. So it's back to business.
Never mind that there's a man bleeding in the hall-
way. Who can possibly fill in writing foodie questions to keep *Shoot the Chef* going at such short
notice?

MADELINE BEAN, of course.

In Hollywood, it's all about being in the right
place at the right time. Maddie is persuaded to
fill in as temporary question-and-answer writer—

continued

just until they can hunt down the show's wayward scribe—and a question-writing star is born.

As Maddie joins the oddball crew of game show pros—which includes a production assistant who raises sheep in the San Fernando Valley, and a contestant coordinator who has found religion—she finds she has a talent for *writing* clues as well as for following them. While keeping up with the show's hectic shooting schedule, dodging a prickly announcer and an amorous prize model, and stepping smack in the middle of a pack of wicked office jealousies, she also uncovers some tantalizing hints as to what really happened to Brad Dart. And after putting up with a star chef who makes the Soup Nazi look tame, she wants to find him fast!

While helping Dara keep the ever more popular game show on the air, Maddie discovers the formula for making Hollywood magic, the secrets of Japanese wasabe smuggling, and how far some people will go to find the right packet of Kool-Aid from 1983, not to mention what really became of her unfortunate predecessor, Brad Dart.

Index